D0426093

BOWHUNTING FOR DEER

BOWHUNTING FOR DEER

H. R. WAMBOLD

THE STACKPOLE COMPANY
HARRISBURG, PENNSYLVANIA

Copyright © 1964 by H. R. WAMBOLD

Revised Reprint, December 1965

ALL RIGHTS RESERVED

Published in Harrisburg by The Stackpole Company

Library of Congress Catalog Card Number: 64-21466

Dedication

To Jim Hamman, an old friend in a little country tavern nestled among the mountains of Sullivan County, Pennsylvania. It was he who encouraged me to write my first short hunting story many years ago. His confidence in my ability led me to a world of pleasure—one offering forms of enjoyment next best to hunting, itself. This is to think and write about it!

Preface

Since Arthur Young and Dr. Saxton Pope revived the bow as a sporting arm early in this century, very little information has been available to help the beginner in this sport.

While Pope's recording of his and Young's early exploits in the hunting field is most pleasantly written in his book *Hunting With Bow and Arrow,* and contains a wealth of information for the newcomer, there has been great progress in methods of hunting and many improvements in equipment since that time.

It is fitting then, and very timely, that Homer Wambold should write this book, *Bowhunting For Deer.*

The Whitetail Deer became accustomed to the sound of the lumberjack's axe and multiplied rapidly because of it. It is the number one target today for big-game hunters with both gun and bow. Not only surviving but thriving in habitat close to man, the deer has developed extremely keen senses which place him at the top of the list as a challenge to those who attempt to hunt him with bow and arrow.

I have reviewed the Wambold manuscript carefully and am delighted to learn that he has explained many of the bowhunter's problems in great detail. His research must have been timeless. I recommend his book to the sage as well as the beginner.

Keep your broadheads razor-sharp. Observe hunter safety rules. Be a good sportsman. Enjoy this book.

FRED BEAR

Introduction

My good wife claims my obsession for hunting has placed me in the category of being a "hunting nut." As the mate to the victim of this incurable addiction, she has become resigned to the inevitable and adapted herself to the role of a hunting widow.

Each fall as the leaves turn into the golden yellows and crimson reds, the crispness of the air beckons the hunter. And as October arrives, a new kind of hunter takes to the big timber and the rolling wooded hills. His quarry is the whitetail buck and doe; his weapon is the bow.

This is a new Nimrod among the many thousands who each year hunt big game. His choice of weapon gives him a chance for closer contact with the outdoors during the balmy Indian Summer days of the autumn season. And truly there are many who have hunted for years with the rifle and killed many a whitetail, who find the change of pace in this form of hunting a challenge so compelling they cannot refuse. Each additional year swells the ranks of our bowhunting sportsmen.

Sound thinking in conservation and game management is providing abundant game for this increasing demand. Of the whitetail hunting prospects today in the United States, my home State Pennsylvania, is rated as one of the best. But elsewhere, whitetails, too, are numerous or on the increase.

In my travels throughout the country to distant hunting grounds, the increasing number of bowhunters is impressive wherever I go. Suffering from the "high cost of living" and the pressures of our modern age of automation, high speed production, and an accelerating space age, hunters take to the hills each fall to relax and enjoy an annual hunting trip. And increasingly, bowhunting is chosen as the most enjoyable form of hunting by many of our country's young men and women upon reaching the age at which they may capably draw a hunting bow and become licensed. This book recognizes such young hunters, and welcomes them to the sport of kings! And, it is primarily intended to tell such budding hunters how to hunt successfully and safely.

I do not claim to be an authority on deer hunting, but rather a fellow hunter who has experienced and observed many things in bowhunting which should prove helpful to others. I have learned that to enjoy bowhunting, one must be armed with both proper theory and practical experience. Knowledge of the proper procedures in pursuing game, and knowledge of the habits and traits of the game hunted as well as possession of skill with the weapon to be employed are all part and parcel of successful bowhunting.

After having hunted over a quarter of a century in many parts of our great nation, I find the old Pennsylvania Dutch expression does hold true, "We get too soon old, and too late schmart!" But the fascination of constantly learning and trying new methods of hunting the whitetail deer makes each year of my hunting more enjoyable.

In order to enjoy bowhunting to the utmost, you must work hard at it. The bowhunter has no choice about this because, the sporting odds which he assumes in this form of hunting are most demanding in terms of individual application and preparation if he is to have a reasonable chance of success.

In 1934, the National Field Archery Association was formed. Later, the various state organizations were organized. Today these related groups cover the entire United States. In recent years archery clubs have been forming at an amazing rate as many seek to master this fascinating sport. But, among the countless archers who participate in this sport, two distinct categories are found. They are those who shoot in competition in regulated sanctioned shoots, and those who have found a new form of hunting enjoyment.

We are here concerned with the *Bowhunter* for deer, his preparation and initial activity in fundamentals, his equipment, and the animal he hunts. Since the whitetail deer is without doubt the big game animal most heavily sought by bowhunters, the text will be devoted to information relating to the habits, traits, methods of hunting, anatomy, and care of game. These topics are of vital importance to the beginning and the veteran bowhunter.

For the one with seasons of past hunting to his credit, the anatomy and blood volume chapters should prove educational, and a decided help.

Since this book is not written with the thought of "professing to know" but instead, "advising how to," no attempt is being made to disqualify the orthodox procedures of bow shooting.

There will be some who will not agree with the contents, and this is a healthy indication of a common interest in the sport. Difference of opinion is based on the experience or background of the individual. There are many who have hunted more years than I, and have collected many varied trophies from all parts of our hunting territories. These are the true "professors" of modern day bowhunting with enriched backgrounds of countless hunting experiences.

May some of the information contained in these pages tend to make your hunting a greater pleasure and the trophies more satisfying.

H. R. W.

Acknowledgements

For their cooperation and help with research I wish to thank: Dr. Mark W. Allam, Dean of the School of Veterinary Medicine, University of Pennsylvania; Dr. John E. Martin, Assistant to the Dean of the School of Veterinary Medicine, University of Pennsylvania; Dr. Monica Reynolds, Assistant Professor of Physiology of the School of Veterinary Medicine, University of Pennsylvania; Gerald E. Eddy, Director of the Department of Conservation, State of Michigan; S. C. Whitlock, Assistant Chief of the Game Division, State of Michigan; Glenn St. Charles, Chairman of the North American Big Game Records Committee, Pope and Young Club; Norman H. Flores*, County Commissioner, Trexler Lehigh County Game Preserve; Warren Wertman, Manager, Trexler Lehigh County Game Preserve; Ed Bond, District Game Protector of Lehigh County, Pennsylvania Game Commission; Harry Keim, Deputy Game Protector of Lehigh County, Pennsylvania Game Commission; Stewart R. Rockwell, D.V.M.; Robert N. Swinehart, a bowhunting companion; Willard T. Johns, former Editor of the "Game News," now of the National Wildlife Federation, Sull-Bow-Buck and the Sullivan County Chamber of Commerce, Pennsylvania.

For their contributions and help my thanks to Don Jacobs, Manager of the Little Lehi Hatchery, Lehigh Fish & Game Association; Allen F. Heller; Albert Williams; Carson Kemp; and Robert Feeley.

*Deceased.

Contents

Chapter

1

The Bowhunter

YEARS ago, the bow and arrow were invented by early men. Just as wheel and fire played an important part in early standards of living, so the bow and arrow likewise shared in elevating man above the level of cave living. Basically a weapon-tool, the bow quickly proved an aid in procuring food. Historians have no doubt but what the bow and arrow played a decisive part in materially advancing the human race.

The first man to put this form of weapon to use plundered and pillaged other tribes for food and clothing as well as for women to bear his offspring. Archaeologists have discovered cave drawings establishing the use of the bow as a hunting weapon some ten thousand years ago. Other authorities claim evidence that these were used even earlier.

Before control of fire to provide warmth, people died at relatively early ages because of exposure. The wheel, however, made it possible to move materials and build shelters in sunny or more suitable terrain, far better suited for human existence than were the damp interiors of earlier used stone or cliffside caves. The bow, too, was beneficial. It made it possible for man to supplement his diet with rich red meat for protein, something sadly lacking in sufficient amounts during the earlier stick and stone-throwing ages. The game killed by this new weapon provided hides which could be used as outer clothing to protect the body. Sinew and bone provided the means for additional tools and implements as well as for smaller weapons. As men persisted, small villages were formed, and finally small states, then nations. As the small nations increased, so did a cycle of plunder continue in greater proportions. Nations fought nations as armies were formed to bring new food-producing land under control or to exploit the conquering urges of the leaders.

As we review more recent history, we see times when the archer had become the bulwark in the military might of nations. The Egyptians boasted many of the greatest archers of early times. The Asian races also excelled in bow shooting; the Persians were most prominent. As the use of this weapon spread among other lands, chapters of European history were moulded through the exploits of Turkish and other famous bowmen.

England seems to have attained perhaps the most glorified and colorful place in the annals of archery history. The short bow, which had been in use for centuries, was an effective weapon in the hands of the Norman invaders of the British Isles at the Battle of Hastings in 1066. William the Conqueror also had a new and even more effective weapon at Hastings—the crossbow. The crossbow soon was widely used throughout Europe, making its greatest reputation in the Crusades.

The longbow, primarily an English weapon, eventually displaced the crossbow about the 13th Century and became the English national weapon. The longbow, five to six feet in length, was pulled to the ear and was therefore more powerful than earlier bows. It was superior to the crossbow because of its higher rate of fire, greater range, and because in wet weather the bowstring could be protected more easily. The clothyard arrow of the longbow was highly effective against horses and could penetrate mail but not plate armor.

In 1300 a most colorful figure in archery history emerged to become a legend—Robin Hood, symbol of the longbow. And, whether this colorful figure did or did not exist as many will argue, England definitely became a country of archers. Every Englishman was required to own a bow and be able to shoot it. Constant competition was held and many, indeed, were the shoots in which trained archers pitted their skill against each other with the new-famous longbow.

Archery played a part even in United States history for we note our American Indians depended upon the bow as a hunting weapon. All too often they also used the bow in warfare against the early white settlers.

Then finally, in 1911, Dr. Saxton Pope, appropriately called the Doctor of Archery, became interested in bow shooting through talking with an Indian patient. Soon becomingly avidly interested in bowhunting, his research and study earned him a place as one of the pioneers of our modern sport. His book, *Hunting with the Bow and Arrow* is still regarded as a reliable source of archery facts and interesting information. Having hunted America, Alaska, and Africa together with his companion Art Young, Dr.

Pope has compiled considerable information of untold value to the serious student of archery.

As a dedication to the memory of these significant pioneer bowhunters the recently organized North American Big Game Competition Club will now be known as the Pope & Young Club. (*See* chapter 20 for full details.)

Another man who contributed much to archery and bowhunting, is Howard Hill. Born in Alabama, November 13, 1900, Hill began shooting the bow at the age of four. Among the enviable records of this "Babe Ruth" of archery are: Winner of seven National Archery Golf Tournaments. He is credited in the Encyclopedia Britannica with having pulled the strongest bow drawn, 172 pounds! As a bowhunter he collected trophies of practically every North American game animal as well as many African species. Of the latter, the outstanding was a 12,000-pound rogue elephant. To shoot it he employed a 125-pound bow, one arrow making the kill. I had the good fortune of hunting with him in 1959 and 1961 during his first hunts in Pennsylvania.

Among the more recent outstanding bowhunters who are compiling record trophies, is Fred Bear of Grayling, Michigan. Bear is a modest but highly competent bowhunter. Engaged in the manufacture of bows, archery tackle, and equipment, he nevertheless finds time to add more trophies to his fine collection of big game animals each year. Of his many record trophies taken with the bow, without any doubt two are outstanding: his Kodiak bear killed during the spring of 1959 with one arrow (1)—the hide squared ten feet—and (2) the India tiger killed at 80 yards with one arrow, a huge man-eating cat that weighed 300 pounds. These are indeed emphatic examples of the deadliness of the bow in the hands of an experienced bowman! Since these trophies were preceded by others, as grizzly bear, black bear, elk, caribou, moose, mountain sheep and goat, antelope, and mule deer, it is plain that his achievements rank him as a top contender for today's title of "Mr. Bowhunter."

Though like other groups, veteran bowhunters will often have varied opinions on many things, there is one fact upon which they are generally agreed. This is that, in hunting with the bow, the hunter must have ability and skill to face unpredictable conditions. He must be able to apply the benefits of practice in every conceivable shooting position and knowledge of both the anatomy and temperament of game is an important part of any successful hunt. With development of the skills of archery prowess and an ability to predict actions of the quarry, a man will become a highly competent bowhunter.

Hunting with the bow offers one challenging year 'round activity and a varied calendar of hunting events: bowfishing in the spring as the carp work the shallows, and woodchuck during the summer months, both elusive and wary targets. In the fall, upland game furnishes a variety of sport with wing shooting having top billing. Then the big game seasons open with whitetail deer and black bear calling the bowhunter into the big timber. For those able to travel widely, every species of wild game found on our continent offers hunting sport of incomparable pleasure. Add to this occasional practice session that every sincere bowhunter needs to retain top shooting form and you can see that your bow will never accumulate any dust!

Unfortunately, the bowhunter has been the target of considerable public ridicule and discussion in recent years. Much of this originates from the ranks of rifle-toting sportsmen. In general, the rifle hunter claims that the bow is not a proper weapon for killing whitetails. He further contends that many deer survive the special archery seasons only to roam the woods with arrows still sticking in their bodies, and to suffer a prolonged and painfully lingering death.

And there are other individuals who have seen fit to join the crusade against the bowhunter. Surprisingly enough, these form a group who do not hunt, or who never have hunted! Then there is also the proverbial individual who contends that hunting is a cruel and vicious sport; he feels that cameras should be the only weapon allowed for shooting the whitetail. Most of these groups insist that the arrow is a cruel weapon. With an air of authority they claim that intense and unnecessary pain and suffering result when an animal is hit by a hunting arrow.

In all fairness to those who term hunting a cruel and vicious sport, every sensible hunter must admit that killing involves a certain amount of cruelty. But only the meat hunter, poacher, or game outlaw can truly be placed in the category of "killer," for his sole purpose and pleasure is found in bringing about the final death of the animal he pursues, whereas the true sportsman hunter (whether he uses gun or bow) finds more enjoyment in anticipating and planning the hunt, the companionship of fellow hunters, and the satisfaction of outwitting his quarry. The greater the odds in favor of the game, the higher the satisfaction of the hunt. The actual kill is an anticlimax of the hunt—by far *not* the greatest thrill the hunter derives from his sport.

In so many cases when the hunter approaches the fallen buck, a feeling of sadness grips him as he admires the fine animal. I am sure many real sportsmen will admit such sentiment in their hunting.

Statements issued by the Game Commissions of both Pennsylvania and Michigan and supported by thorough investigation, assure everyone that allegations that there are deer running around with arrows still sticking in them are without foundation and that this is usually merely hearsay or unfounded rumor. Every state that permits a special archery season has found the conduct of the hunter, kill of game, percentage of game lost, etc., satisfactory and within satisfactory proportions.

Without any question the bowhunter has earned the respect of his fellow sportsmen. He has borne the brunt of opposition with few, if any, black marks against his record. More and more rifle hunters are becoming bowhunters too or accepting the bowhunter. Decreasing criticism clearly indicates that archery has earned its place among hunting methods considered proper and sporting.

I must admit that when starting to hunt with the bow, the most attractive feature to me was that this was a means of getting more deer hunting under my belt in one season. Hunting whitetails and other big game animals is my favorite activity using both rifle and bow, as the season permits. But after having tagged my first buck with the bow, I have found a greater fascination in this form of hunting. There is more thrill and satisfaction in getting my deer with the added handicap of this weapon. Though I have shot my share of deer with the rifle, and still regard myself as an avid "powder burner," I find bowhunting far more rewarding and relaxing.

I am willing to bet that one of the reasons for the lessening cries of protest against bowhunting by the rifle hunters is the fact that more and more of them are giving bowhunting a try and they like what they sample. Finding it harder than they assumed was the case, they are rising to its challenge and determined to master the sport. This, of course, applies only to those hunters who regard a game animal as a trophy, not to those who see game only as a number of steaks and roast jumping along! Meat hunters may get thin hunting with the bow! The conversion of many rifle hunters to bowhunting accounts for the increasing number of bow hunters we see each year.

Rifle hunters have found that the bowhunter is not really harming or interfering with general hunting conditions, nor is the special "pre-season" archery hunting adverse to game. They have also learned that the "any sex" or "hunter's choice" privileges allowed the archer does not put any serious dent in the deer herd. As a matter of fact, the final figures on total reported kill show an extremely low percentage of deer bagged by the bowhunter in any given season.

In Pennsylvania the total deer kill on the highways during any given year exceeds the kill by bowhunters. For example, the total kill of deer by bowhunters amounted to 1,358 deer in 1958, 1,409 in 1959, and 1,174 for the 1960 season, whereas the deer kill on Pennsylvania highways totalled 7,047 in 1959, and 7,187 in 1960. This clearly indicates that highway traffic is taking a greater toll of our deer herds—not legal bowhunting seasons or generous bag limits!

Just what type of individual is the average bowhunter? Why does he place himself at such a disadvantage weapon-wise? What added personal satisfaction does he get out of this method of hunting compared to the conventional hunter with firearms?

Most of the more experienced and successful bowhunters are converted riflemen. The added handicaps peculiar to bowhunting are attractive to many hunters who have been successful on big game with the rifle. As so many of us have learned, the mere act of killing a fine game animal eventually loses some of its appeal. With the coming of scoped rifles and flat-shooting calibers, hunting has become a matter of spotting the game, taking a firm hold, and applying a steady trigger squeeze. Stalking and outwitting game with the rifle is no longer, in fact, necessary. Therefore the end result is less satisfying than it used to be.

When the hunter decides to try his hand at bowhunting, he is embarking on a venture that will require much of his time, but which will provide him with relaxation and a wholesome pastime year 'round. Skill with the bow is not achieved overnight; it requires constant practice. The bowhunter must discipline himself towards the perfectly coordinated shooting form. He must develop the skill of an instinctive judgment of distance to a degree that he may apply it in all types of terrain and weather. Becoming thoroughly familiar with his equipment is a "must" for every bowhunter. Without this familiarity he cannot expect to achieve or keep the consistency and smoothness demanded for flawless shooting form.

In comparing the amount of practice required of the bowhunter with the rifleman each year, I would say the following is typical. The average hunter may fire twenty rounds through his favorite deer rifle before the opening day of the season. He will usually do this a few weeks before the opening day, sometimes not until he arrives at camp. But the average bowhunter will shoot from one hundred to two hundred arrows per week during the greater part of the year. Conservatively figuring, we can say that the average archer fires seventy-five hundred shots prior to the opening day of his season. Why does he do this? Because he has to constantly try to develop a higher degree of accuracy with the bow. At the same time he must try to overcome the many faults which creep in to jeopardize accuracy. Repetition—constant practice—is the only means of developing perfect coordination and flawless release. The bowhunter may be compared to the golfer or bowler. Each requires constant practice to achieve and maintain top skill in the sport. The man who plays golf twice a year can't expect to break one hundred. The archer who does not work hard at his shooting year 'round usually does not get to use his big game tag!

Even after achieving a fair degree of skill in handling and shooting the bow, the bowhunter finds other problems to contend with when hunting. The effective range of his weapon is limited. Terrain and cover offer few openings through which his arrow must pass to get to the game. This means he must get closer to his game than his rifle-toting cousin. So he must master the art of stalking and patient waiting. He learns the art of natural camouflage, and develops an ability to remain motionless for long periods while the deer are within sight but not in range. The bowhunter never finds the same shot presenting itself twice. He must get his arrow through thicket, brush, and timber. In many cases, he has deer within twenty yards but cannot shoot because of heavy intervening cover.

In contrast to the rifle hunter when he has made his shot and hit or missed, the bowhunter may not have another chance. He must wait and see—"sweat"—until his game comes within closer range. But many times the deer will turn and pass out of range despite an excruciating ten minutes of quiet waiting by the hunter with ready bow! Patience is a definite "must" for any successful bowhunter. Game is not easy to come by in most cases. And when the final moment does arrive and the buck is within range, the bowhunter is usually sweated by several minutes of waiting and all tensed for the shot. He must release his arrow smoothly, get the arrow through available openings in the timber. He must have judged his distance properly. He must put his arrow into a vital part of the target—not just anywhere in the deer. This is quite a bit to remember compared to merely raising a rifle, placing the crosshairs on the front shoulder of the deer and squeezing! Without any doubt the bowhunter has more misses than the rifleman. Final kill reports for any given season will verify that fact. But at the same time the bowhunter works harder than the rifleman in making those misses!

The bowhunter must learn more of the country in which he hunts than the rifle hunter. In most cases he will cover more territory than the rifle hunter. He must know the main "travel trails" of the deer from their bedding to feeding grounds. He must know more about the habits and traits of the whitetail so he can anticipate moves the deer will make. Because he has the advantage of a quiet weapon, he is often able to intercept a deer for a possible second arrow after an initial miss. Knowing the terrain, he can figure which way the deer will move, then get ahead of the deer and be posted and ready for another try. But this maneuver has to be done without imitating a bull moose crashing through the timber!

A special season for the bowhunter is a necessity in order that he has a fair chance at this quarry. If he had to hunt in direct competition with the rifle hunter, he would be greatly handicapped in getting within effective range, since the deer would become too alarmed and "spooked" by rifle fire. Safety is another reason demanding a special season for the bowhunter. Since the bowhunter must resort to camouflage he cannot risk the chance of being shot for a deer while concealed in brush or on low limbs of a tree stand.

When final kill tabulations are made each season, the number of deer tagged is extremely low when compared to the number of special archery licenses sold. The bowhunter's success ratio is far below that of the rifle hunters, but his morale is higher and his attitude still optimistic! Why does the bowhunter accept this low percentage of success more favorably? Simply because he starts his hunt with a full knowledge of the handicaps he has assumed and continues hunting fully aware that his chances of filling his tag are against him–about fifty to one. But his attitude is because of the personal satisfaction and pleasure he finds in bowhunting. It is far beyond that offered by any other form of hunting.

The bowhunter is a sincere follower of his sport. He is well represented in state departments as well as in the local sportsmen's clubs. He provides responsible support for bowhunting through membership in various state and national organizations. He takes an active part in their programs. Interested in all the various phases of hunting, he thinks of conservation, proper conduct, respect for the property of others, and consideration of his fellow sportsman's safety. Having survived much unfair ridicule and criticism by other sportsmen with quiet restraint, he has now earned their respect and recognition.

Positive proof concerning the complete capability of the bow as a big game weapon has accrued throughout our North American and African hunting grounds. Such famous bowhunters as Howard Hill, Fred Bear, and many others have collected trophies that are the envy of many a rifle-toting sportsman. These big game trophies vary from upland game to the largest and most dangerous of species such as the grizzly and Kodiak bear, elephant and lion, as well as many other species whose taking was long considered possible only with long-range rifles.

These examples of the efficiency and killing power of the hunting arrow on all forms of big game are entirely conclusive. When properly placed, the arrow is as effective as any rifle bullet.

2

Choosing Your Bow

WHEN your decision to try bowhunting becomes a reality, the choice of basic tackle is your first and most important step.

The processes of learning how to handle and shoot the bow, do not require deluxe models of equipment which sell in the higher price bracket. One fact must be emphatically stressed at this point to every budding bow bender: *No degree of skill and accuracy can be purchased with a bow.* These must be developed through advanced shooting practice. So dismiss the thought right here that the fancy recurve with the high price tag will make you a better shot! Very few individuals are natural bow shots—long periods of practice are necessary to develop consistent accuracy.

For the beginning bowhunter the choice of bow should be among the lower priced models. This is advised to allow for interest after a trial period without extreme expenditure. After having attained a fair degree of skill and accuracy with your weapon, changes in equipment can be made according to personal likes and physical capabilities.

The basic components needed to start your initial bow shooting are relatively simple and inexpensive. A reliable straight bow made by a reputable manufacturer can be purchased for less than twenty dollars. Add a half-dozen arrows (target type) for an additional four dollars. A shooting tab or glove, plus an arm guard will complete your initial needs. The total investment will not be more than thirty dollars, and your equipment will be entirely adequate for a proper start in bow shooting. Extras that you might add to your initial outfit are: quiver, additional arrows, and extra bow strings. Although helpful, these are not absolutely necessary at this stage of your training.

It would be very wise of the beginner to reserve some of his funds for later expenditure on equipment. Rest assured that for a while you will be replacing your supply of arrows quite frequently. I shall never forget my first time around a twenty-eight target field course at our local club. I started with ten of my original, first-dozen shafts. When I walked away from the twenty-eighth butt, I was arrowless. I had broken every shaft while going around. Today, happily, I can shoot around with four arrows.

My first bow was a straight end, solid glass, a shoulder-jarring job of sixty-pounds draw. I still have the bow and usually pack it along as a spare on hunting trips.

Your first bow should not have too heavy a draw weight, for this will only bring on the problem of "drawing fatigue." A good way to pick draw weight for that first bow is to take one that you seem to draw without any apparent effort. Since there are many fundamentals to be learned and habits to be formed, the added distraction of an extremely heavy drawing weight should be avoided. Draw weights of thirty-five to forty pounds are about the very maximum for a start, and the spine of the arrows should match.

The bow you choose should be constructed of modern wood core with fiberglass overlay. This will provide the most cast with the least drawing exertion. It is not necessary to limit the choice of your first bow to a straight-end type; this is advised solely from a cost standpoint. But if you purchase a more costly recurve, your initial shooting results will be no different.

The three most common types of bows available in today's sporting goods stores or archery tackle shops are straight end, reflex or partial recurve, and the full-working recurve.

Of these, the straight end will be the least expensive due to its simple manufacture, and the full working recurve will have the highest price tag. The latter's manufacturing process is more detailed and complicated, hence the higher price. But with bowhunting as our ultimate goal, we must keep in mind that no one quality brand bow has more killing power than another.

Let me advise at this point that you should avoid thinking of buying inferior bows. Remember when you went to buy that first deer rifle? No one could have sold you a new rifle for $9.95 because you knew that such a rifle would lack the quality and workmanship needed for top performance. You wanted only the best so you insisted on one of the leading and reputable makes. Apply this same sound reasoning when you go to buy that first bow. There are many reputable manufacturers who offer a line of bows, all top-line equipment. Buy from the reliable manufacturers.

Avoid the thoughts of buying some "Deerslayer" outfit, complete in a box with bow, arrows, and tab and arm guard for $9.95, or some other low bargain price. Above all do not buy your equipment from some bargain house or super market! *Buy only a reliable brand from a reliable dealer,* for he specializes in archery tackle and his product is backed by a reputable manufacturer. Such a dealer's advice is sound, especially since most archery tackle shop owners are bow shooters themselves. Inferior tackle at ridiculous bargain prices spells only trouble with a capital "T"—dangerous to the shooter using it, and to others in his immediate area. If you try to hunt with such "free box-top equipment," the chances are that you will succeed only in wounding your game and losing it.

The full working recurve bow is a bit more touchy in shooting than the straight-end model. This is due to the design of the limbs. Upon examining a recurve you will find a string groove

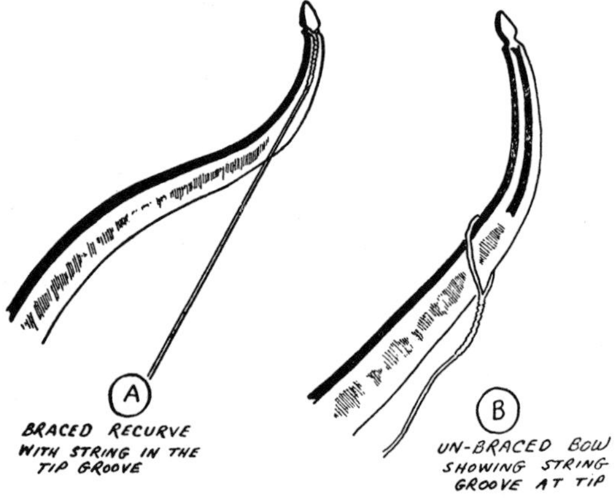

extending from each tip for several inches. When the bow is strung and braced, the string will lay in this groove adjacent to the points where the sweep of the bow limbs curve away from the string line.

Improper holding of the bow will cause the limbs to reflect error. Such errors become magnified through the action of the string groove bearing points at the upper and lower limbs. In these circumstances the beginner is likely to compound his shot scattering. Therefore, in most cases the straight-end bow is desirable to start with, since it will reflect less error and result in tighter grouping. Despite this, there are those who shoot a recurve bow for tournaments, where accuracy is the most important factor.

Recurves draw easier than straight-end bows. The design of their limbs accounts for this. During the draw, the limbs of the bow are being bent by the backward pull of the bowstring while the bowhand holds the center of the bow in a stationary forward position. The straight-end bow requires constant pulling until the fullest extent of the draw is reached at the anchor point, whereas the recurve bow demands a full-strength pull only to a certain point beyond which a form of "coasting action" sets in until full-draw position is reached.

Straight-end bows are more rugged than others in design. They permit rougher handling. They are less vulnerable to developing twisted limbs through stringing difficulties. Very few cases of a set in a limb develop in straight-end bows, though this problem is quite common in the full-working recurves. When you compare the two types of bows you will see why this is the case.

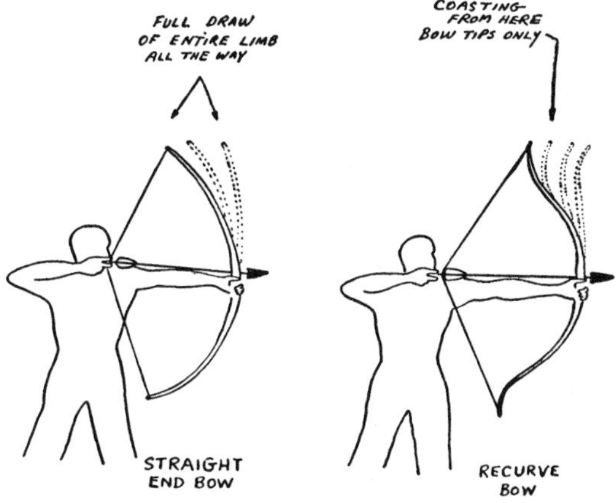

A straight-end bow has heavier limbs with less taper. When unstrung, you can grasp the bow at the tip of one of the limbs; it will require quite a bit of strength to twist the limb to any degree. But if you were to do the same to a recurve bow, you would find the limbs quite flexible and easily twisted to either side because of the extreme taper from grip to tip. *Caution:* do not attempt this test on a new recurve. Let an experienced bowman show you, instead. An inexperienced hand making such a test can ruin a new bow.

In archery talk, a straight end has "build up" or "stacking" in the last stage of the draw. This property is determined by the design of the bow limbs, especially by the degree of taper and cross sectional dimensions. When the bow is drawn to the anchor point, "stacking" or "build up" becomes evident because of the constant effort which must be exerted to reach full draw. In contrast, the recurve bow may be drawn all the way with a smoother pressure "build up," no stacking, throughout the draw due to its shape and the extreme taper of its limbs. In hunting, the straight end provides more power in short range shots, but on the other hand it is limited in ability to cast the flat shooting trajectory needed on long shots.

The overall length of hunting bows is important. Good maneuverability in thicket and timber demands that a bow have short limbs, but only to the point where no undue sacrifice results in performance and handling in shooting. You should be cautious when choosing the short version of hunting bows. At the same time the distance between the limb tips is decreased in the draw, the angle of the bowstring becomes quite acute, especially at the full draw position. This extreme acuteness of angle evolves at the nocking point on the bowstring. When an arrow is nocked and fully drawn, it will cause a pinching of the fingers of the drawing hand. True, there are several short hunting bows available which feature smooth drawing actions without stacking, and a minimum of string pinching. Though such bows are extremely fast and powerful, only the seasoned bowhunter is capable of using them with consistent accuracy.

The longer the limbs, the smoother the action of the bow; the shorter the limbs, the more the bow's recoil is increased. The short hunting versions have a jarring recoil, and never permit long sessions of practice. Average bow lengths are around sixty inches. Modern design combined with today's materials and the skills of the bowyers have made it possible to incorporate all the wanted features in standard bow lengths. These include smooth drawing action and handling, maximum cast and power, minimum stacking and little string pinching. Overall size does not present a maneuvering problem of any concern to the average bowhunter.

Here some useful comparisons can be made for rifle hunters who intend to try their hand at bowshooting. Carbine barrels, due to their shorter length, limit the distance and accuracy of such rifles. The longer rifle barrel increases the weapon's range as well as its accuracy. The effects of various bow lengths are somewhat comparable to rifle barrel lengths. Short bows limit accuracy and range, while longer bow lengths permit increased range and a greater accuracy. Another comparison may be offered. The recurve bow compares somewhat with the faster calibers such as the .250/3000, .257, and the .270. It is a high speed, flat shooting weapon with maximum range. The straight end bow compares with heavier and slower calibers such as the .35 Remington, .348 Winchester, or the .300 Savage. Its performance features slower velocity, an increased trajectory, and it has a limited range. Ignoring the disproportionate ranges between bow and high power rifle, we can say as we might of rifles, that the straight-end bow could be classified a short-range weapon, and the recurve bow a long-range weapon.

Now all rifle hunters have their pet calibers which they swear by and with which they get good results. Likewise, bowhunters are much the same; some of them swear by the straight-end bow, while others claim the recurve is superior. An example of this is evident in the cases of two of our outstanding bowhunters.

Howard Hill sticks by the long bow (or straight end) with which he has killed most big game species. He is also an advocate of heavy tackle for hunting all game, for maximum penetration and bone-smashing power. He recommends close-range shots if at all possible, thereby applying the maximum power from the bow.

Another outstanding bowhunter, Fred Bear, prefers the full recurve bow. Having killed most big game species, he also advocates heavy tackle. But he prefers the recurve to assure minimum trajectory and flat shooting at slightly longer ranges than practicable with the flat bow. He, too, recommends shots at ranges within forty yards or less for maximum accuracy and employment of the full power of the bow. So it is clear that arguments concerning which kind of bow is best often conclude in a stalemate.

3

Arrows

AFTER you select and purchase your first bow, the next and equally important component of your weapon is the arrow. Let's emphasize again that the spine of the arrow should match the power of the bow. Unless this is the case, your shooting will be erratic and possibly dangerous.

To explain briefly, the shaft of all arrows must have a certain amount of flexibility. This flexibility, or lack of it, is termed the "spine" of the arrow. Spine is the property which enables the arrow to recover from the bending and initial oscillation, which initially occurs when it is shot from a bow. As the arrow is released the bow string imparts a forward propelling force, casting the arrow into flight. As the arrow leaves the rest on the bow it bends, due to the force exerted by the bowstring and bow limbs, actually making a curve around the front of the bow as it leaves in flight. Correct spine will compensate and bring the arrow back into proper line of flight. This proper flight is the line of sighting from bow to target.

Paradox is the term used to describe the ballistic curve of the arrow when fired from the bow. It is similar in many ways to the ballistic curve of the bullet when fired from a rifle.

If the spine is not right, recovery will be subject to more or less reaction. Weak spine will cause extreme paradox, while over-spined arrows will never complete the paradox recovery curve. This will result in shots going to the right or left of the area intended to be hit. Proper spine of the arrow will assure recovery in paradox, sending the arrow along the flight path as sighted and held, for proper hits.

Note of caution: Since underspined arrows flex or bend beyond proper proportions, if shot from a bow too heavy in poundage, the results can be dangerous to the shooter. In such cases the force of propelling action of the bowstring can flex such a shaft to the breaking point, as it leaves the bow. The rear end of this shaft can imbed itself into the bow arm of the archer, resulting in painful and sometimes serious injury. *Never attempt to shoot any arrow in your bow without being sure of the spine test; avoid a hand flexing test to judge any shaft!*

Cheap arrows, commonly called "barrel arrows," do not have any spine check. But most arrows of grades above that of barrel arrows are spined in relation to various bow weights. The cost of arrows will vary depending on locale and demand. Most

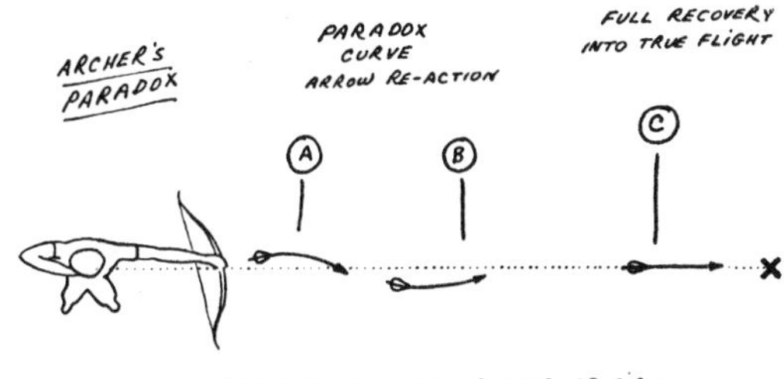

archery tackle manufacturers make spined and matched arrows in both target and hunting heads. The average cost of such arrows for target use is about one dollar apiece.

The length of an arrow is determined by your individual drawing measurements. This is similar, in some respects to your individual sleeve length—the shorter the arm, the shorter the arrow, and vice versa. Reliable archery tackle shops have a measuring device with which they can determine the proper length arrow for your personal proportions. Most bows are rated in pounds of drawing weight at 28-inch draw, unless otherwise marked. The average individual draws a 28-inch arrow. When a shorter arrow than normal is used the draw weight of the bow is lowered and when longer arrows than the 28-inch are used in the same bow its draw weight is increased.

Many bows will have their maximum drawing length tagged. Dismiss the thought that the longest possible draw adds anything to your possible capabilities as an archer. An arrow of 28-inch length is more stable in flight than longer shafts. This is due to the flight characteristics of an arrow. Whenever possible, the shooter should try to develop skill with shafts of the standard 28-inch length.

An interesting fact about a bow is that when it is drawn to 28 inches, it is ninety-nine percent close to the breaking point! Thus it can readily be understood that longer draw cannot possibly coax appreciable amounts of extra power out of it. (There are, of course, exceptions such as when the shooter's physical build includes arms of extreme length. When this is the case, he must use a longer shaft; but we are concerned only with average arm length.) If the average bow were to permit overdrawing (beyond twenty-eight inches by shooters of average arm length), shooters might compromise the position of their bowarms, thus actually decrease the desirable distance between bow and anchor point.

In proper shooting procedure, form release, etc., is taught to the archer who intends to go in for competition. Locking of the bowarm is stressed as proper; so is the direction in which the toes should point, plus other details. Practically the same procedure in the basic training of archers is followed as that in instruction for rifle shooting, especially if the rifle shooter will compete in bench or range matches. Prone positions must be assumed in a prescribed manner, the sling must be applied in certain ways, and trigger-squeeze must be precisely synchronized with breathing. The development of the right basic habits and training in the proper etiquette are fine whether it be of rifle shooters or the archer—providing it involves shooting at artificial targets in special set aside areas.

The big game hunter cannot always apply all the steps of proper form and shooting stance in the field. Therefore he must adapt himself to the terrain, the movement of the target, and be prepared to take an immediate effective shooting position, all within a matter of seconds. In most cases he must shoot from some extremely unorthodox position at any moment. This demands some short cuts or deviation from proper procedures as stated "in the book."

One of the short cuts for the bowhunter involves his bowarm position. Avoiding the locked arm method, the elbow is bent, bringing the shoulder forward into the span between the arrow nock and bow position. This reduces the total span between both points and allows for two things, a quicker draw, and shorter drawing length. This is a useful tip for the bowhunter who can draw around thirty inches since this span he can control or limit his draw to twenty-eight inches. This avoids overdrawing such as might occur when under the stress of stalking game. By developing this shooting form for hunting, he can draw a normal 28-inch arrow and use the shaft length proved most stable in flight.

The standard fletching on most arrows is three feathers. Fletching stabilizes the arrow in flight. For the rifleman the following comparison can be made. Inside the rifle barrel the twisting rifling lands cause rotation of the bullet as it passes through the barrel and leaves the muzzle. This rotation of the bullet gives it a stabilization in flight. It permits the bullet to reach the intended target without gyrating or wobbling. The same rotation keeps the bullet on course.

The fletching on an arrow does the same for the bowhunter as the rifling does for the rifle hunter. It causes the arrow to rotate in flight and provides stabilization. This rotation is controlled by the "set" or spiral in design of fletching. Without such fletching, the arrow would have a tendency to turn end over end in flight; even if it didn't, it would certainly deviate to one side or the other of the target.

Now we come to the choice of fletching, and the desirable amount of feathers. To keep things as simple as possible, the beginner is advised to stick to the use of arrows with the conventional three-feather fletch. Later, he can change or experiment on abstractions and wildcats. Factory arrows come with the standard three-feather fletching, still the most effective and time-tested arrow in hunting. Howard Hill uses a three-feather fletch with maximum spiral twist. Fred Bear makes three-feather fletched arrows as the regular hunting arrows for the archery tackle market. He uses the three-feathered fletch with the maximum twist. But numerous variations are to be found in use among the many archers who experiment with "wild cat" designs in arrow fletching.

Going from the stabilizing end to the business end of the arrow, we now are confronted with a choice of heads.

In the choice of hunting heads, more commonly known as broadheads, we again find a wide variety of shapes and designs. Of the various shapes and designs some are extreme. Others are "Rube Goldbergs," and some are "wild cat" in performance and characteristics. The basic broadhead is a two-blade tip. The three-blade head is sometimes called the bodkin tip. With the imagination and ingenuity of today's bowhunters, it does not seem to take long for new designs to appear on the market.

One of these innovations is the four-blade version of the original bodkin head, basically conceived with the idea that the fourth additional cutting edge will induce more profuse hemorrhaging. The razor-insert head has also become available to bowhunters. Some have a permanent insert, while others allow the insert to be used, or the arrow to be shot without one. The insert, smaller in size than the basic two-blade cutting edges of the tip, provides additional cutting edges giving the shooter his choice of either a two or four-blade tip. This razor-type head has become very popular among bowhunters and results in the field on all types of game have been highly favorable.

The design of some hunting tips permits rapier penetration, with cutting edges and point honed to razor-keen sharpness. Other heads are designed for their bone-breaking capabilities. A few heads offer both maximum penetrative abilities as well as the strength necessary for rib cutting or chest-bone penetration. The physical construction of these two types of heads usually differs. The head for maximum penetration is long and needle-pointed. In many cases, the ferrule to which the cutting edges of metal are attached is plastic. Such types can be classed as two-piece construction with the ferrule as one unit, and the cutting edges as the second unit.

There are also some two-piece heads which feature a metal ferrule to which the cutting edges are attached. And some types employ the all-in-one construction in which the head is one unit consisting of both cutting edges and ferrule. Of the many types of hunting heads available, some have superior flight characteristics. Others are extremely heavy, causing trajectory problems.

As in rifle hunting, the bowhunter has many "wildcat" designs to choose from in available hunting heads. Each has features claimed to make it more deadly. Some of these heads have been used by bowhunters and such heads have killed deer. In most cases such a typical "wildcat" head has been used by the designer himself; it then appears on the market and is available to the bowhunting ranks. Of such extreme designs, the following examples are of particular interest.

The scissor-type head is rather unique in design and action. Shot in a closed position, it opens into a razor-sharp cutting head as it penetrates. Some bowhunting buddies with whom I hunted in New York have used this head and killed deer with it. They are staunch supporters of the design and carry them every hunting season. But my personal opinion is that some malfunction may possibly occur in the scissor action when it hits a deer. This could result in a crippled or possibly lost trophy. I prefer basic head design to avoid the possibility of any such problem.

Avoid broadheads with long slender points; in many cases the point will curl upon contact with bone. Too many hunters, incidentally, use dull heads. Before hunting, make sure your blades are razor sharp. Carry a small hone while hunting and keep them that way.

The important thing to make sure of when choosing the hunting arrowtip is performance in flight. The type and weight of bow as well as the length of arrow to be used have a lot to do with the performance of any given hunting head. Heavy poundage in a hunting bow delivers extreme thrust to the arrow and propels arrows with heavy tipped arrowheads quite accurately. In contrast, the lighter bow will have less propelling force causing the same heavy headed arrow to drop considerably. This will shorten the distance in which the bow can be depended on to shoot flat or its point blank range. By the same token, the heavyweight bow will cause certain heads to wind-plane or yaw in flight, whereas the lighterweight bow will cast this same head in perfectly normal flight.

Every bowhunter owes it to himself to try various heads on a target. By experimenting, one can find the type head which will give the uniformity, the most stable flight, and the greatest accuracy.

When the right choice has been made, little if any difference will be noted in performance between a field-tipped practice arrow and the hunting arrow used.

The next tip test involves game in actual hunting. The tip's effectiveness in penetration, blood vessel cutting, and ability to penetrate bone and muscle will determine how good your choice has been. The hunter using a heavier bow shooting two-blade heads will obtain maximum penetration. In such combinations, a common occurrence is to shoot arrows completely through game. Since the arrow should cut as many blood vessels as possible, the one that passes completely through the game does the most effective job. This can also be accomplished by the light bow user simply by combining arrows proper in spine, fletching, and hunting heads.

Generally speaking, four blade heads do twice the damage that two blade heads do and their penetration is considered to be superior since the "X" hole relieves pinching on the shaft. Some authorities definitely feel that single bladed heads should not be used on big game, only three or four bladed heads.

When you have decided on a hunting head and proved its performance by sufficient practice shooting, you are ready to purchase your hunting arrows. These arrows should be uniformly spined and matched to assure top performance. It is good practice to try each and every hunting arrow on a practice butt. This checks the shooting action or grouping of each shaft.

If, for example, you purchase a dozen arrows, mark four of them with consecutive numerals from one to four. Then, at the maximum point blank range of your bow, shoot the first four arrows in the sequence marked. Try to duplicate each shot as closely as possible, then check for grouping. If you find one arrow that does not cut the black after three or four group shootings, mark it with an "X" and go to the next group of four. Marking each set of four as before. Continue until you have test fired, identified and separated the erratic shafts in all three groups.

Suppose, now that you have test fired your dozen arrows, you find that seven group tightly in the black while the other five group around the outer edge of the five ring. These five arrows have been marked with an "X" so that you can tell them from the others.

You now apply a permanent marking to these erratic arrows so they will be easy to spot. This can be accomplished by adding another cresting band, or by coating your cresting with a solid color, or by putting a dab of paint on the nocks. Now that you can spot these five arrows immediately, they are ready to be kept in reserve. When you hit the timber for the hunt, you are loaded with seven shafts that will shoot a tight group. If the hunting is good, with plenty of shooting, you have to dig out the reserve supply. If and when you do so, you will be prepared, for you know from the test shooting that these five arrows shoot a larger group, in most cases either right or left. Now you adjust your hold to compensate for use of the reserve arrows and make good hits! Without having checked beforehand, firing such arrows at a random game target could mean a bad hit, or even a miss!

One note of caution. After having test fired your arrows to check the grouping of each shaft, *sharpen each broadhead before hunting*. A good practice to follow is to sharpen every broadhead after it has been shot. Firing into the ground, rotten stumps, straw butts, etc., will dull the cutting edges of their tips and may bend the points. This should be rectified before any hunting use.

4

The Hypo-Arrow

RECENTLY a hunting arrowhead of unusual design was put into use for the purpose of collecting specimens of deer for biological study. It was formerly fired as a projectile from a compressed air gun. The injection mechanism remains the same insofar as basic function is concerned. The shape of the unit was changed to match the flight characteristics of an arrow.

This head was tried in an experimental hunt conducted by the Southeastern Cooperative Wildlife Disease Study, under the direction of Dr. Frank A. Hayes. Dr. Hayes is the head of this group, and also a professor at the School of Veterinary Medicine at the University of Georgia.

The hypo-arrow tip is about two inches long, cylindrical in shape, and of metal construction. Its five parts are: (1) needle point, (2) outside tube, (3) plunger, (4) firing cap, and (5) the arrow ferrule.

When being assembled for use, the rubber plunger is lubricated and inserted into the tube. Next, the firing cap is inserted behind the rubber plunger and pressed flush with the back end of the tube. The rear of the tube is then sealed by screwing the ferrule socket to the back of the tube. Next place the tube upright on the ferrule end, and place a solution of one millimeter of the drug inside the reservoir. Attach the needle point, thus sealing the front of the tube. The completed unit, when attached to the shaft of an arrow by means of the ferrule socket, is now ready to do its lethal job.

The drug used is succinylcholine chloride. An injection of 50 milligrams dissolved in one millimeter of water will kill any member of the split-hooved species within a few seconds of entering the blood stream. Harmless to humans, however, the drug can be handled without danger. The edibility of the meat of any deer killed with the drug is not affected; it can be consumed so far as the drug is concerned without any adverse after effects or change in taste.

Hunting with this kind of weapon is done in normal fashion, with one exception; hits in the chest area or thoracic cavity are avoided. The archer places his shot either in the front shoulder, high in the back, or in a hind quarter. Since the drug works through absorption into the blood stream, a hit in the chest cavity could slow down the drug's absorption since its dilution with body fluids would reduce it to a harmless state. But a hit in the solid muscular structure, either in the front or hind quarters will, however, assure speedy absorption into the blood stream.

During the experimental hunt, deer were down and dead within 30 seconds of a hit. The arrow does not penetrate beyond the needle tip. It will not stick in the deer, but falls to the ground within a split second after hitting the animal. This short time, however, is sufficient for injection of the drug in full dosage.

As in normal bowhunting, deer must be stalked to close range. Shots are as difficult to make, and all the basic handicaps encountered while bowhunting deer in the usual way exist when using the drug. The only difference is in the results after a hit has been made. Using the drug, the bowhunter can count on a hit meaning a deer either dead within 30 seconds, or down and helpless, with death but a matter of seconds away.

The effectiveness of this chemical killer has many of the rabble rousers and die-hards within the firearms clan working up quite a lather. Past crusades in which certain individuals have persecuted the sport of hunting with the bow, repeatedly have dwelled on the "pin-cushion" deer they asserted were running around in the woods, dying a slow and agonizing death. The appearance of the hypo-arrow in their opinion has provided an answer to this hypothetical condition.

The push is therefore on to legalize the hypo-arrow for bowhunting. However, this is not the wish of the archer, but rather the work of some prejudiced riflemen who insist that bowhunting is a cruel, vicious, and a very unsportsmanlike method of hunting deer. Their concern in bringing about this allegedly foolproof method of hunting with the bow for an element of hunting of which they are no part, is very touching indeed. It seems odd to me that such emphasis is being placed on the few unrecovered deer left in the woods during archery hunting seasons while no attention is being focused at all on the problem of reducing the thousands of crippled and dying deer left in the woods each year after the rifle hunting seasons are over.

Could it possibly be that this attitude represents a fear of a relatively new shooting sport changing all our thinking about how to shoot deer? They say it is hard to teach an old dog new tricks. After a lifetime of using an old and familiar shooting tool which, if pointed at some general area of a deer, will impart a paralyzing shock to stop the animal, why start all over again with a shooting tool that demands new background, and additional training? The cry is quite familiar by this time—bowhunting is not sportsmanlike!

No, the bowhunter cannot begin to kill animals at fantastic ranges of hundreds of yards. This requires no great skill in stalking, no patience in waiting for game, no acute knowledge of wind currents, nor the ability to accept frustration when the deer although close, cannot be taken. Long-range shooting with a rifle requires only a limited degree of skill with the weapon, spotting of game at long distances, and making the kill.

If rifle hunters had to depend on placing a single shot in a precise and vital point on a deer instead of depending on firepower and a paralyzing shock factor to drop all the deer harvested during a given rifle season; the total kill would drop to an amazingly low figure! This is not the viewpoint of a purist, but that of a hunter who has and still does hunt with both the rifle and the bow. And I know what the score is, after the annual hunting seasons are over.

The sudden appearance of the .270, .300, and 7mm Magnums among the rifle hunters in deer country indicates that less hunting and more shooting is desired by such individuals. I sure would like to know what these super-gunned hunters are after, elephants—or whitetail deer?

To be fair to all, let us weigh both sides of the chemical weapon's hunting potentials. Remember, personal recreation and relaxation in the outdoors should be uppermost in the minds of all who hunt. So, what is the most fascinating part of hunting? The challenge of the hunt, is the only logical answer. This covers the multitude of things which taken all together, make a man eager to match his skill and wits against the wiliness of the whitetail deer.

Many hours of repeated practice never leave an archer with a sense of false security. He knows from past hunting experiences that his skill with the bow can still stand improvement. But how many rifle hunters will admit that they should put in a bit more practice with their favorite rifle?

The challenge of learning the habits of the deer and developing a skill whereby the hunter can guess what the whitetail's next move will be is one that requires participation. Learning about wildlife and game habits has always been a highly interesting pastime. Yet how many rifle hunters will go to the trouble of learning about the deer? Why should the rifle hunter bother when he can rely on others to push the deer within shooting range?

The bowhunter has the challenge of knowing that no matter how skillful he is with the bow on the target course, placing an arrow in a vital area in certain kinds of terrain or cover may prove impossible; all too often this is the case with the deer as close as within 50 feet of the bowhunter. The challenge of such frustrations which most bowhunters encounter is tempered by the challenging need for patience, a quality which every bowhunter must possess in order to enjoy his sport. What greater challenge could a hunter face than to have a deer within a stone's throw and still be unable to make a killing shot? Only great patience will keep the bowhunter returning day after day in hope of better luck.

There's also a challenge to make that arrow count, knowing well that a poorly placed shot will result in an unrecovered deer. This, too, is an important part of bowhunting. No sincere bowhunter ever questions the fact that some deer are lost each archery season. Losing game after having wounded it is a part of all hunting, whether it be rifle or bow. Too much is being said about this fact on the one side, and not enough is being mentioned about it on the other.

Personal satisfaction plays a far greater part in the sport of hunting than many realize. There are two sides to what an individual enjoys from a personal standpoint. There is the man who gets a real kick out of outwitting a sly whitetail buck, catching the deer with its guard down. Regardless of whether he makes a kill or not, he has been satisfied with a successful stalk. But the other man is the one who, unless he makes a kill, cannot return from a hunt without feeling cheated.

Personal satisfaction is found by many in other ways. Many a hunter finds enjoyment in the quiet solitude of the big woods or the chatter of the busy squirrel. Some find the colorful leaves of an autumn woods a real scenic pleasure. And let us not forget that warm midday lull when the deer are not moving. A drink of cool water from the small stream, a sandwich and a relaxing smoke, and that pleasant short outdoor nap in the warm afternoon sun—ever stop to think how much of this would be missing if one killed the first deer seen on each hunt?

The day you start carrying hypo-arrows, you will find the hours so pleasantly spent to be far fewer. That deer within 50 feet that you could not possibly hit in a vital area with a regular hunting arrow now cannot get away. You will merely plunk your needle-tipped shaft into any part of the body you can get it to, and a minute later you will have your deer.

The darker side of hypo-arrow hunting is the undeniable fact that such a hunting tool would change the entire sport of bowhunting. The sale of archery licenses would climb sky-high throughout all whitetail areas. Non-hunters would try their hand at hunting with a bow, for no degree of skill would then be needed to get a deer. All that would be required would be for the hunter to get fairly close, then hit the deer most anywhere. Results would be almost guaranteed, a sure kill if hit.

Tracking a deer carrying an arrow in a vital spot is often such a problem as to be the nemesis of many of today's bowhunters. Many archers who hunt each year are incapable of following and recovering such wounded deer. In order for such novices to recover their deer, blood sign must be plentiful. I have a friend, for example, with whom I have enjoyed many bowhunts in the past. He has shot a number of deer with his bow. But should this friend forget to mow his lawn for several weeks, I could lose him right in his own back yard! And remember that the deer wounded with a hypo-arrow will leave no blood trails whatsoever.

Another point. How far can a deer travel in 30 seconds? Whitetail deer have been said to be capable of speeds up to 30 miles per hour. This means that the deer could cover 158,400 feet in an hour, or in one minute, 2,640 feet. Dividing that in half, we find that in 30 seconds the deer would cover 1,320 feet, or 440 yards. This, of course, is calculated at the top speed of the animal. So let's be fair and assume that the deer will make an escape flight at half that speed. I am sure that many a bowhunter has watched a deer leave the locale where shot at about 15 miles per hour. Thus our deer is capable of covering well over 200 yards before it might fall a victim to the quick-acting hypo-arrow. Then add a terrain of dense cover, typical of most whitetail country. This includes laurel thicket, hemlock, or scrub oak, so you might have a real problem.

Or, let's be lenient and cut down the distance such a deer will run after being hit to, say, 100 yards. I am sorry to say, in complete disagreement with those who lack any appreciable knowledge of bowhunting but insist that the hypo-arrow is the answer to unrecovered deer; they are wrong. We will not thus solve the problem of unrecovered deer. And I also know a lot of rifle hunters who could not find a deer within 100 yards if there was no blood trail or snow on the ground to help tracking and recovery.

The hypo-arrow experiment, as conducted and publicized in the article I saw, was staged in terrain that consisted of mature timber stands. The photographs illustrating the hunt showed open forest, no small brush, but plenty of openings through which a bowhunter could shoot for distances up to 100 yards. The fact is, I question that any hunter-fearing whitetail would be so foolish as to venture into such open areas. Could it be that the deer were there because they were baited or lured into this open area? The lack of any browse or other deer feed could be clearly noted in the photographs. No, I've hunted too many years to believe that deer will feed in an area as open as the middle of Yankee Stadium on a clear and sunny day! At least our whitetails in Pennsylvania don't relish this type of cover; they avoid it.

I can also vouch for whitetails from New York, New Jersey, Maine, New Brunswick, Nova Scotia, Ontario, Wyoming, and Montana as having a similar dislike for "picnic grove" feeding grounds. Also, I noticed that the bowhunter illustrated in the photographs could not find a branch lower than 20 feet on which to fasten a shooting platform, so he had to lash it to a tree trunk, six feet above the ground.

I would sure like this group to try for our Pennsy whitetails in that manner. We have deer that would spot that bowhunter in his tree platform in such open timber from as far away as 100 yards. Then all they'd do would be to snort, circle around, and pussy-foot off into the thickets.

Therefore, I say that every bowhunter should carefully consider any suggestions which promise a new Utopia for bowhunting. First, consider the source of the article, what background the writer has in bowhunting. Second, consider the motive for the article. Third, compare the proposed substitute with the present hunting method being used. Be fair when you list each side of the question and remember to look at it strictly from an unprejudiced viewpoint. If the proposed change is to be any good, your personal satisfaction from bowhunting must be enlarged and the entire sport of bowhunting must be bettered by the change. So now after you have carefully considered the hypo-arrow, if you find the aspect of "shooting fish in a barrel" appealing and sporting, remember that you ought no longer to call yourself a bowhunter. Instead, maybe some new title such as "bowkiller" might be more pertinent.

5

Quivers

IF YOU decide to add a quiver to your initial outfit, consider the type you choose carefully. Of the many kinds available today, there are mainly three basic designs: shoulder quivers, bow quivers, and pocket or belt quivers.

Shoulder quivers, designed to be worn over the shoulder, require the wearers to make an "over the shoulder" arrow-drawing arc, quiver to bow. The off the shoulder variation involves an "around the shoulder" arrow-drawing arc, while the back quiver variation necessitates a choice of either an "over the shoulder" or an "around the waist" arrow-drawing arc.

As with most archery equipment, agility in efficiently using the quiver selected *must be developed by the bowhunter.*

The design, materials used, and quality vary from the plain working model quiver to the gaudy Roy Rogers versions bedecked with fringe and spangles. Some feature extra pockets to carry personal items, hunting knives, etc., and some look very much like a super deluxe golf bag for midgets. It is wise to shy away from fancy designs and quivers with added extras; pick a simple design instead. Your rule should be to not pack more weight than necessary. The basic purpose of the quiver is to carry additional arrows, so don't end up carrying a miniature foot locker on your back!

If a back quiver is to be your choice, stick to a workable simple job. Look for such features as quality leather for durability, ample room for at least eight arrows, good workmanship in the stitching and the carrying strap. Especially look to see that the quiver provides adequate protection for your hunting heads.

My personal choice in *back* or *shoulder quivers* is the Howard Hill model. Reasons for this choice are its simplicity of design, the adequate room for as many as a dozen hunting arrows, and the fact that it still permits free drawing room without shaft crowding. This quiver is made of top-grade saddle-skirt leather and the leather has a chrome tanned oil finish affording durability that should last a lifetime. It also has a built-in double bottom, and an extra outer layer of leather around the bottom to assure proper support in carrying the hunting heads. This quiver is actually worn "off the shoulder," but an "around the shoulder" drawing arc may be used—an advantage when there is little headroom. I use it when hunting brushy or thicketed country, especially when I expect to be away from my base operating point for the day.

With one exception, there are no auxiliary pockets. A small leather sheath of the same material as the quiver is attached for carrying an extra bowstring. I have packed such items as a plastic rain jacket, spare sweater, or lunch in such a quiver on past hunts simply by stowing them in the quiver with the shafts.

Another type of quiver is the bow quiver. Basically it is designed to carry only three or four extra arrows. Comparatively less in cost than the shoulder quiver, it carries both the bow and extra arrows as one unit. For my money, there is no quiver that permits faster withdrawal of an arrow with less movement. The drawing arc with such a quiver is completed within the length of your shaft. Nor is overhead room any problem with this quiver, for if it is possible to get your bow into a shooting position, it is also possible to draw an arrow.

There are many types and versions of the bow quiver on the market today. Some are excellent in design and construction, and some merely provide a way of carrying extra arrows. A bow quiver of proper design and construction must incorporate certain features if it is to function properly. Its construction must be lightweight without sacrifice of strength. It must attach to the bow in a manner that will permit shooting without any interference to the sighting picture, and it must not get in the way of the bowstring when the latter is released. Neither must it interfere with the action of the bow limbs when an arrow is loosed. And, not only must it not interfere with this action, it must also remain in such position as will permit an immediate draw of a successive arrow.

The bow quiver must be constructed of the right combination of materials to provide durability and resistance to weather.

Attachment methods should permit easy removal of components without the necessity of special tools or gadgets. And, of course, the method of attachment should be such as will not injure the bow or mar or deface its appearance.

The most important function of any quiver is that it must adequately protect the hunter from the hunting heads. There are many "Rube Goldberg" quivers on the market which completely neglect safety! In fact, many expose the arrowheads while they are in a carrying position!

If you are interested in this kind of quiver, consider the matter of protecting the arrowheads, however. Frankly, the heads have less protection in this model and are apt to require frequent sharpening. There is also a safety factor to consider.

My personal feelings regarding such quivers is that they should be outlawed by the individual state game departments. Having your bow equipped with such an exposed-heads quiver is the same as walking around in the woods with a handful of sharp but unsheathed hunting knives! I am sure no sane man would enjoy trying this. One slip or stumble while working along your way could inflict severe injury to some part of your body.

Consider the following maneuver common in hunting: While stalking a deer, your attention is focused on the animal as you slowly work your way within range and shooting position. You move in a crouched position, bow in ready position with the arrow nocked. Suddenly, an overhead branch appears in your path and you duck. Depending on the position of the bow, you might ram those exposed heads into your face or eye!

I once saw a bowhunter incur a severely lacerated hand during a wild boar hunt several years ago. We were gathered waiting for the drive to be organized, and the man had imbibed a concoction to such an extent that he "had to go." Since there were ladies in the group, he had to move out and step behind a hemlock. Calling to a companion, he asked him to hold his bow while he attended to other matters. As this companion reached for the bow, he grabbed it at the point where the exposed heads were clustered around the upper limb. The result was extremely painful to the victim who suffered sharp hand cuts. This held up the hunt considerably. The injured bowhunter had to leave the hunt, since his hand bled so profusely a pressure bandage was required to prevent extreme loss of blood.

But I also watched another bowhunter experience a more humorous accident one season. This hunter had one of the two-piece bow quivers on his bow; it was loaded with very sharp, lethal hunting arrows. We had made a slow, silent drive on a small island. Finally the deer were bottled up at the lower end. As we expected, the deer then made a break to escape across the shallow water behind us. A nice doe bounded up in front of my hunting companion but skidded to a stop as his first arrow missed, sticking in the ground in front of her. Quickly fumbling for a second arrow, he managed somehow to get one out of his quiver contraption and into position for a second try. But what he hadn't noticed in his excitement of getting the arrow out of the quiver, was that he had twisted the balance of the shafts, always a possibility with such a two-piece arrangement. One of the units had twisted, thus turning one broadhead directly in the path of the bowstring!

Watching him miss his first shot, then draw a second arrow with all the reactions of a normally excited hunter, I waited to see if he would get a hit before the doe bounded away. My position was such that I could plainly see both the deer and the hunter.

He drew and released his second arrow as the doe snorted and bounded into the thicket. I could not see any arrow in flight, although I thought he might have made a hit. Then his irreverent remarks reached my ears. As he had released his second arrow, the string was neatly severed by the broadhead which had twisted into its path. His arrow had imbedded itself in a tree about twenty feet in front of him, but it had gone at least five feet to the right of intended flight path!

Reaching his side I saw the unbraced bow in his hand and first I surmised that his bowstring had torn. He remarked about the severe jar he felt in his shoulder when the bow had unbraced, and he still was in a state of surprise over the events. Examining the bowstring, we found it cut as cleanly as any knife could have done. The arrow was next retrieved and the bow thoroughly examined for possible cracks or breakage. But, luckily, the bow had withstood its phenomenal shock and held in one piece!

After a bit of gabbing and restringing his bow, we stopped to analyze what possible serious outcome could have resulted from this accident. After thoughtfully considering the more serious things that could have happened, all laughs were gone and we had a feeling of comparative relief. Removing his bow quiver contraption right there, he stowed his extra shafts in my shoulder quiver. That night he drove into a nearby town and bought a more reliable bow quiver to complete his hunting week.

My personal choice of *bow quiver,* now used for many years, is the model made by the Bear Archery Company. Whenever I intend to do any tree hunting, I attach this bow quiver, load it with four extra shafts, and head for my hunting area. In my bowhunting over the past years in many states I have observed more of these quivers on bows than any other make. This is at least one sign of their popular acceptance.

The Bear bow quiver offers every feature that should be found in a properly designed and constructed quiver of this type. It is constructed of materials that provide strength, proper counteraction against bow action in arrow release, and has the needed ruggedness for durable wear and resistance to weather. Simple in design and strictly functional, it features secure locking of shafts during carry. It enables crisp and smooth drawing action without distortion of the original bow position. Light in weight, it is no added burden when the bow is attached and loaded. Properly positioned, it does not conflict with the sighting picture nor does it interfere with the path of string release.

Equally important, it features a built-in protective metal cover located at the head end of the quiver; *the hunting heads are completely protected from any contact with the bowhunter* while it's carried or handled. For my money, this is the fastest drawing bow quiver that you can buy. With very little practice, anyone can become quite adept and fast with this quiver. This is an important factor when facing a whitetail!

This quiver is available in three types of mounting. I prefer the bolt-on kind. A brass bushing is inserted into the bow handle at a designated point. (The bushing is furnished.) The quiver is then attached and removed by means of a single screw which has a slotted head which can be turned with a coin. The other model is exactly the same in construction, but has a tape-on attaching feature. This one mounts on the bow at two points, bearing on upper and lower limbs close to the grip. It is attached and removed through use of masking or friction tape. The latest "snap-on" bow quiver is mounted on the bow with a spring clamping arrangement. It goes on or off in seconds and does not mar the bow finish.

A third category of quivers includes both pocket and belt quivers. Pocket quivers are indeed used by some hunters, but such quivers are not basically suited for hunting. They are more properly designed for field shooting on target courses and they should be confined to such use.

Belt quivers are preferred by those bowhunters wanting plenty of room in drawing an arrow. While it is claimed that other quiver styles permit better maneuverability in brush and thicket, I find no real fault with the belt quiver, at least not insofar as concerns its safety, durability, or easy arrow withdrawal. But I should add that those who choose this type of quiver are likely to find it at its best in tree hunting.

Regardless of the quiver you choose, take the time to learn to handle it properly. Be sure your choice features *adequate protection* for the hunter! Then you may expect to use it for many enjoyable hunts.

6

Accessories and Tips

A NOTICEABLY fine thing about bowhunters is the fact that whenever two or more of them get together, they hardly ever seem starved for conversational topics. Whether the discussion concerns equipment, habits of game, methods of stalking, or deals with their educational experiences in the woods, bowhunters as a rule are willing to share their lore with others of the clan. In the same vein, here are some odds and ends of information which can be classified as of at least "fringe area" interest to most bowhunters.

Nocking Points

A nocking point is placed on the serving of a bowstring to help the hunter nock each arrow at the same point or "zeroed in" place, each time. As usual, there are several ways of providing for this. Here is how you can make a simple and very effective nock point for your hunting bow:

With dental floss, wrap a ball on the serving directly above the proper nocking position on the string. Build this ball high enough so that it will act as a stop. If properly made, the nock will not be able to move beyond its correct position on the string because of the ball. With the ball placed above the nocking point, the arrow is mounted low on the string and then slid up against the ball.

The illustrated nocking method will enable any archer to nock his arrow without glancing at the string. While watching a game animal, he places an arrow on the bowstring, sliding it up until it rests against the ball. Then he is all set to draw and shoot.

Broadhead Edges

Two kinds of broadhead edges seem most often used by bowhunters. One preference is for the honed razor-edge, sharpened much the same way as knives, except that the final edges must be more carefully finished. But others prefer a serrated edge, depending on it to exert a more effective jagged cutting or tearing action. For the latter edge, use a file in sharpening.

The case for or against each shape must be judged by the individual hunter. Those who advocate the honed razor-edge

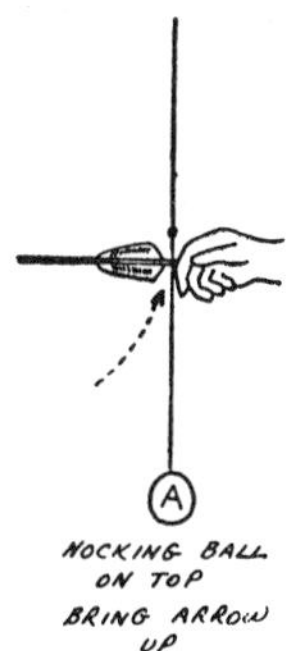

claim for it more penetration than is likely to be achieved with the serrated edge. But many hunters prefer the serrated edge, believing that its hacksaw action will cut more blood vessels than will the razor-edge's.

Bow Covers, Brush Buttons

Optional and inexpensive accessories helpful to the bowhunter are numerous. Bow covers reduce the reflecting glare of bow surfaces, and protect the bow from scratches. Moreover, they enhance the hunter's camouflage as well. As an alternative, many hunters depend upon ordinary mud to eliminate glare.

Brush buttons avoid the tip-clogging of bowstrings, a condition often caused by brush or small twigs. Moreover, as the hunter moves through the woods, brush buttons protect the bow against becoming caught as otherwise often happens when the tips are carelessly exposed to branches or heavy brush.

String Silencers

Special string silencers are used to eliminate the "game-spooking" twang of the bowstring when an arrow is released. You can easily make effective string silencers yourself. Use two rubber bands of ⅛-inch thickness. Cut the loops, then tie each strip about three inches in from the end of the bowstring. Use a simple loop knot and leave equal lengths of the strips dangling. Such silencers do a fine job.

Tip Protectors

Rubber tip protectors for the lower limb keep the lower string loop in place and protect the tip as well in ordinary use.

Arrow Holders

Arrow holders keep the arrow in a "ready" position, nocked and on the arrow rest. A slight tension on the bowstring locks the arrow in the holder until released when the bowstring is drawn. Spring action flips the holder out of the arrow's way. This is an excellent gadget for the tree hunter. It enables you to hang your bow on a convenient branch stub or place it across a branch loaded and ready to draw when game is sighted.

Tree Seats

Among the helpful accessories for bowhunters, several can be constructed by the bowhunter, himself. One such "do-it-yourself" gadget is a tree seat. I designed and made one several years ago and have used it many times. Primarily intended for tree hunting, it is equally useful on the ground.

In a tree watch, one of the discomforts is awkward footing and the constant problem of trying to find a better position for resting tired muscles. The tree seat provides the comfort sought and lets the hunter occasionally take his weight off his feet. In such a seat, cramped muscles can relax while at the same time the hunter avoids distracting tensions such as build up if awkward tree positions are maintained for prolonged periods. After several hours standing or leaning in a cramped position in an otherwise good tree watch, this seat will look worth its weight in gold. Its cost is very low, and its simple design takes little of your time and effort.

List of Tree Seat Materials

1 pc. Plywood (or ¾-inch white pine), 8 x 17 inches
26 ft. Sash cord, or other line strong enough to support your weight safely
2 ea. Rings, 1¼-inch diameter, of at least ⅛-inch stock (Be sure the rings are the solid rather than the split kind)
3 ea. Snaffle hooks, 3-inch
1 ea. Clincher loop (open)
2 ea. Swivel loops (closed)

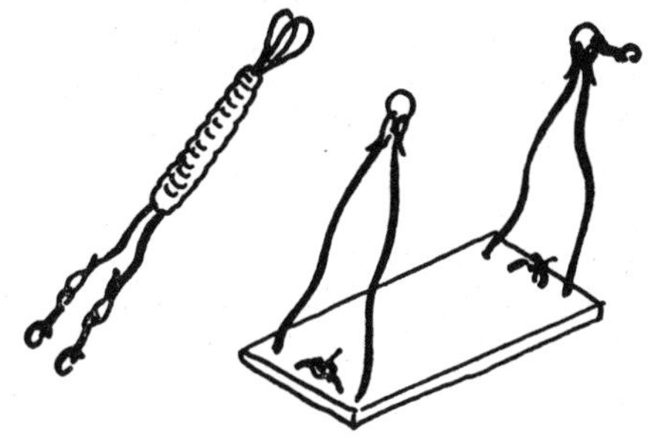

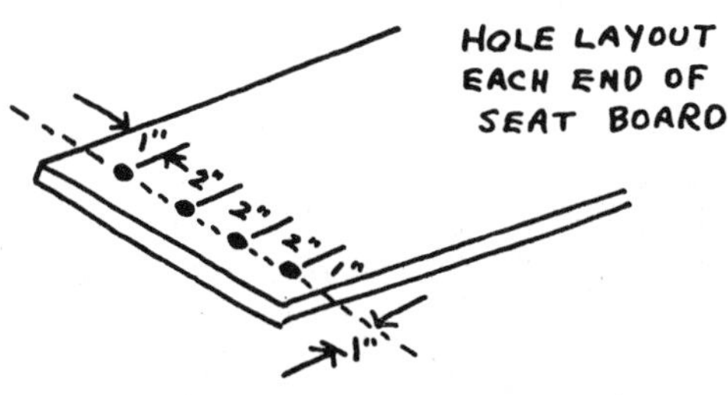

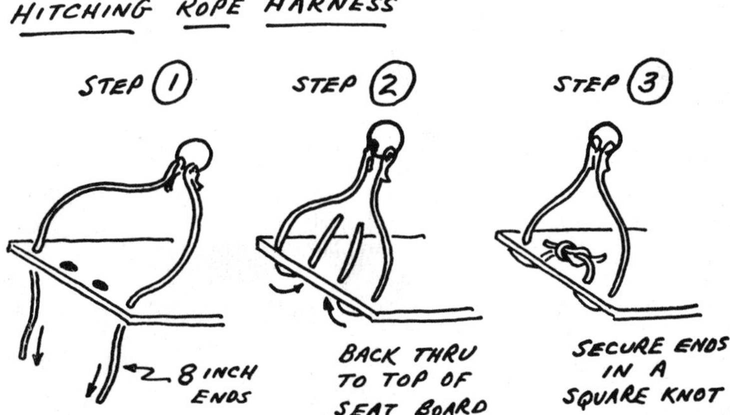

Steps for Assembling the Tree Seat

(1) First drill the eight holes (¼-inch diameter or larger as necessary to fit cord) required for attaching the rope harness. Locate the holes as shown in the drawing.

(2) Cut two lengths of the line; make each one four feet long.

(3) Secure each cord to a ring by bringing its ends together, then inserting the opposite (or doubled) end of the cord through the ring thus forming a loop through which its two loose ends may be drawn. Now each ring is securely fastened to the middle of a cord by a slipknot.

(4) Mate the dangling ends of each cord to an end of the seat board. Thread the lines down through the outer holes, then return them up at the same end of the seat, using the middle holes. Now tie each set of cord ends securely with a square knot.

(5) Next, attach one snaffle hook to one of the two rings (either one) and close the clincher loop for permanent attachment. Only one hook is needed for engaging the other ring handily in wrapping or carrying, etc. The cords may now be wrapped around the seat and the side harnesses hooked in carrying.

(6) Attach a snaffle hook to each end of the remaining 18-foot length of cord. Use the two swivel loops now, if desired. (*Note:* In fastening these, I used a double loop and two half-hitches. The loose ends of the cord should be taped or spliced to the main line.)

Using the Tree Seat

The seat can be easily packed by *wearing* it across the small of the back. Wear the harness ropes as a belt; let a snaffle hook simulate your belt buckle. Or, by locking the two side harnesses together in front, you can carry the rig with the longer separate line attached to one of the rings. Most of the time, the long line is looped and wrapped for carrying right along with the seat.

By making a timber-hitch wrap with the long line around the trunk of a tree, the seat can be rigged for comfort in ground hunting.

If an overhead branch of sufficient size and strength is available, the seat can be rigged like the old-fashioned swing. (Figure B.)

At times I have rigged the tree seat solely to stand on, thus avoiding the cramped positions encountered in deep tree crotches. (Figure C.)

A lightweight camper's hatchet can be attached to the bottom of the seat; fasten its sheath to the underside. Mount the hatchet in a carrying position, the handle to be down and across the center of the buttocks when the seat is worn.

The hatchet accessory is helpful in clearing away obstructing dead branches when you are in a tree watch, and also useful

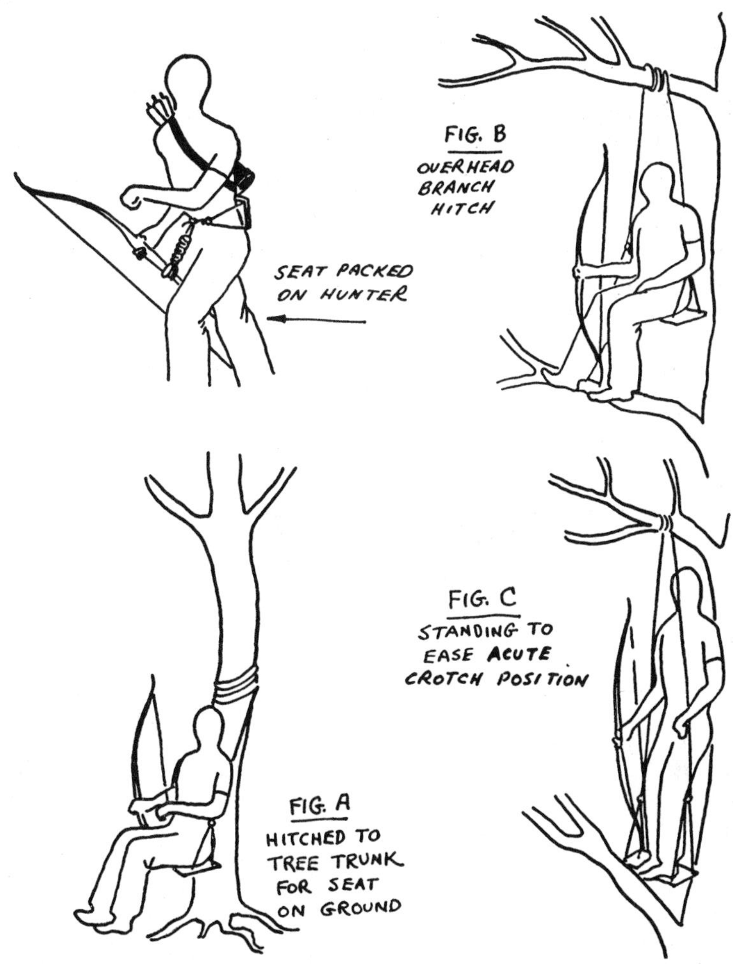

in cutting a pole for carrying your deer. A hunting knife in a sheath can be substituted for the hatchet in the same way. Either the hatchet or the knife is worth every bit of its weight and the small room it takes in your hunting gear.

Scented Game Lures

If you feel that an animal scent or "buck lure" may help your hunting, here is a way of using it without bringing the odor from the outdoors into the car or cabin with you. Tape a small puff of cotton to the inner face of your lower bow limb. Saturate this cotton ball with your favorite "anti-B.O." scent and go hunting. When you get back to your car or camp that evening, remove this cotton puff and leave it outside until the next day when you can put it back on the bow for hunting. Tomorrow maybe it will need a slight recharging, but apart from that, you'll be in business.

Tools for Field Repairs

A simple kit that will enable you to make minor field repairs can be carried in a small compact container. The tools and other items listed below are sufficient for changing heads, replacing broken or cracked nocks, for wrapping a nocking point on a new string, sharpening broadheads, and repairing damaged fletching.

Quantity	*Item*
1	Mill file (flat), ⅛-inch, with shank broken off and taped for handling protection.
1	Duco cement, tube
1	Ferrule cement, stick
1	Candle stub
1	Pliers, slip-joint style
1	Dispenser, dental floss
6	Pins, common
3	Broadheads, spare
6	Nocks, spare
—	Extra bowstrings

All of the listed items will fit in an ordinary cigar box or in a small metal box of similar size. Such a kit takes very little room in your gear and is very handy in camp.

Bowhunter's Kit Bag

Some personal articles must be carried on a hunting trip but the bowhunter will be wise to keep them at a minimum. The following articles are desirable and of such little bulk that they may even be stowed in the pockets:

Compass and small topographic map of the quadrangle being hunted, if the territory is strange to the hunter; hunting knife; twenty feet of nylon rope or light sash cord; waterproof container filled with wooden matches; extra bowstring; small slip-joint pliers; extra handkerchief (large red bandanna); two chocolate bars; and a small plastic bag.

Nothing need be said in defense of the compass and the "topo" map as "must" items for the hunter bound for strange country;

the important thing is that he know how to use each properly. The light rope has many uses. Upon working myself up into the branches of a tree, I have used such a line many times for hoisting my bow. Matches without a doubt are vital to the hunter and should be carried at all times. They should be weather protected in a waterproof container. The red bandanna has many uses; it can be a handy sling in case of arm injuries or it can form a compress or head bandage in a pinch. The pliers will help in removing broadheads from tree trunks and in repairing bent arrowpoints. No bowman goes into the woods without an extra bowstring. The candy bars serve as reserve food in event of a forced night in the timber; they are also welcome when the hunter is on a stand. The small plastic bag, if you are lucky, will do nicely for your trophy's heart and liver.

7

Common Sense and Safety

FROM the safety standpoint, bowhunting enjoys a good reputation. Possibly this is because the shooting hazards in bowhunting are confined to relatively short ranges. Maybe the fact that most bowhunters try to aim at game with equal or greater exactitude than they would in using a gun contributes to bowhunting safety records. Admittedly the longer range hunting rifle extends a danger radius over a far larger disk of timber than does the hunting bow. Perhaps the bowhunter's quiver helps, too, the weight and creaking of its deadly contents constantly reminding the hunter of the need for safety at every step. But whatever the factors may be, the accidental shooting injury rate among bowhunters remains low. So when you bowhunt be sure you too do your part to continue this fine record.

This means you must be sure you *see* your target before loosing an arrow, and that you must never draw any arrow unless you are *facing* a target. Respect the potential danger of straying arrows, whether they be hunting broadheads, field points, or rubber blunts. And at all times conduct yourself with the highest regard for the safety of others and with every consideration of their property rights.

In roving the fields and woods, never walk with an arrow nocked in shooting position. When a hunter who does this slips or falls, it often means another case which must be tabulated as a "self-inflicted injury." Remember, too, it isn't just arrowheads that cause injuries; cracked arrow nocks may likewise do so. Also shafts will sometimes break, their jagged ends causing injuries ultimately to be reflected in statistics.

Recall earlier admonitions concerning the need for precautions when carrying arrows in quivers. It bears repeating. Extra hunting arrows should always be carried in a quiver that protects the hunter from the arrows' business ends! And never carry extra hunting arrows in your hip pocket. A buttocks wound can be extremely painful; it can even terminate your hunting for a whole season. This, incidentally, is one of the toughest parts of the body in which to control hemorrhage, especially when a person is alone. Walking certainly only aggravates such a wound, thus making control of bleeding difficult.

When retrieving arrows that missed, employ the proper procedure. Always examine the shaft carefully for cracks or splits; never put the arrow back in the quiver without this thorough check. If a shaft is split, you should learn about it before a second shot. If you don't, you'll be lucky to get the arrow out of your bow in one piece. Then, even if you succeed it is likely to fly erratically and such an arrow is unlikely to have a chance for penetration upon striking game. Remember, too, that split or cracked shafts have a tendency to explode when they are released. The fletched end of the shaft may drive forward into the shooter's arm; the jagged end of the shaft may implant crippling splinters.

It is common-sense safety to check shooting equipment constantly. Watch your bowstring for fraying, the bow limbs for cracking, and the glass backing for parting. Also watch arrows for shaft splitting or cracking, and inspect carefully for cracked nocks. Remember, when you hunt you will usually be in remote country. Fellow hunters will likely be few and far between. In such locales the lone and injured hunter simply cannot expect to get help from others. Consider the terrain you will have to cover in order to get back to your camp or car; realize just how serious an accident can be some distance away from possible help. Avoid the many unhappy possibilities by always practicing safety rules and using common sense.

Bowhunting is attracting many new followers, many with little or no experience as woodsmen. Perhaps this suggests why each year more bowhunters seem to get lost than is the case with rifle hunters. Some bowhunters even get so deeply engrossed in stalking or tracking game that they neglect to keep their bearings. Wounded deer will often lead a hunter in confusing paths; if you lose your bearings in following such a deer, don't panic. Consult your "topo" map and use your compass to establish your location. If you made a good hit the chances are that your deer will not lead you far from a familiar spot. With some back-tracking you can usually return quickly to a familiar area.

In the rare case when you might be unable to find your way back to camp before dark, resolve to make an overnight stay right there in the field. While daylight permits, gather plenty of firewood. Because weather during bowhunting seasons is usually quite moderate, a hunter's exposure to the elements for one or even several nights in an emergency should pose no real serious health problem. Make yourself comfortable and relax as much as possible. An all-night fire will provide both comfort and a good beacon for searchers. Convince yourself that you are in no great or immediate danger and try to get some sleep; after all, think of the dandy story you'll be able to tell your grandchildren about the night you had to spend alone in the big woods! When dawn comes you can resume your search for familiar surroundings.

But never try to travel wooded mountainous terrain at night. This involves too much of a gamble with falls and perhaps serious injury. The not uncommon result of such folly is a badly battered hunter, his face and clothing unnecessarily chastised by the branches and brush which harass night wanderings.

A temporarily lost hunter is much wiser in "staying put" for the night. And if you ever believe you are lost, even in the daytime, don't hesitate to swallow your pride and call out occasionally. Thus you may be heard by someone hunting close by, unknown to you. Keep in mind, too, that someone may be out looking for you. If they should be, your periodic calls will help him locate you.

A very wise rule to follow in all hunting, of course, is never to hunt alone. However, if, hunting alone is your choice (many do), always first inform someone of the general area in which you intend to hunt. Always take the time to do this so that if you are not back within a reasonable time a search is bound to follow. It's just common sense and insures you against either of the two most common problems, the lost hunter or the injured hunter.

Apart from other injuries which sometimes handicap a hunter's movements, foot blisters are so common they deserve special comment. If you develop a bad blister while hunting some distance from your car or camp, the best bet may be to remove your shoe or boot and make your return either barefooted or in your stocking feet. This is not the ideal way to travel, of course, but in some cases it is the best solution. You'll have to reconcile yourself to making slower time on the return trip.

A bowhunter's footgear is very important. Proper fit of footgear is necessary to avoid discomfort and fatigue. Tight shoes prevent good circulation; shoes too loose invite blisters. In choosing footgear for hunting, select those which support the ankles properly and which have soles that will provide good traction in any weather, wet or dry. Avoid unnecessarily heavy winter footgear or insulated boots, for example, since as a bowhunter you are not likely to encounter the severe weather for which they are designed. Your boots need not be waterproof, for that matter, either.

Concerning bowhunting apparel in general, the most common fault that I have observed is that too many hunters overdress. Often, a number of inexperienced hunters will tire early in the day simply because they are wearing too many heavy garments. In the generally mild bowhunting seasons there is no real need for heavy woolen socks, insulated boots, and other items perhaps appropriate during the later rifle hunting seasons. Instead, loose-fitting lightweight garments are best. They don't have excessive bulk to handicap movement nor induce heavy perspiration. After all, the bowhunter is an active fellow who will usually move around enough so that he should be able to stay warm with lighter apparel.

Unfortunately, the overdressed hunter is apt to feel cold and clammy when he undertakes a tree watch especially after perspiring travel for several hours through the woods. Under these circumstances, I would rather be slightly chilly but still dry. And needless to say, if you are fortunate enough to get a deer to pack back to camp, you will be glad to be lightly dressed. Even then, the chances are you will shed some of your "light attire" before you get your trophy back!

8

Knowledge of Game Being Hunted

WHEN entering strange hunting country, there are several observations you should make. They may greatly influence the question of whether you will or will not get any shooting. Deer trails form a sort of road map to the experienced and observant hunter. By studying them carefully, he can determine where the deer feed, where they move when seeking bedding grounds, and which routes are the most heavily traveled. Hunting in the right area at the right time of the day spells the difference between seeing game or wasting a day.

Many attribute the scores of certain persistently successful hunters to luck, but I would wager that if one checked the procedures of those successful hunters, he would find them to reflect more "know-how" than pure chance.

The first year I hunted in the Torn Mountain section of New York, just outside White Bear Mountain Park, I walked into relatively strange country. My only advantage was many years of hunting experience. Since deer in New York turned out to be no different from the Pennsylvania whitetails with which I was familiar, I was able to use my earlier acquired deer hunting "know-how" to guide me, even during the first day in the new area.

Studying the trails and runs of the deer that first day, I worked my way along the base of a side ridge, noting especially the places where heavy traveled trails branched up towards the top of the ridge. Finally, I picked one that looked particularly well used and followed it part way up. Then, upon noting that very few feeder trails any longer branched away from or into the main well traveled trail until it reached a main bench quite some distance up the side, I moved back about halfway down and stepped off to the side. Picking what many hunters refer to nebulously as a "likely spot" under a hemlock, I began a watch of the trail, both to my right and of the entire area below me. I was facing east.

Several hours later after the rising sun had made elongated shadows on the forest floor, I spotted the movement of a new shadow in the tall timber below me. Brilliant sun now flooded this area making it easy to detect anything moving. Upon studying the new shadow, I identified a lone deer working along the shallow slopes at the base of the ridge. Since this deer was at least two hundred yards below me, I could not then become very excited about it. Nevertheless, while looking away from time to time to check other surrounding areas, I found my eyes returning to the deer below as it ambled slowly along in the timber.

The deer presently turned and headed uphill. I realized it was gradually coming up the traveled trail and would soon pass my chosen position. Now I was prompted to step slightly out from the hemlock to better watch the run. When the deer came within eighty yards or so of me, I was able to see a rack clearly and distinctly bobbing its way slowly up the slope. A perfectly balanced, ten-point rack adorned this buck's head, each of the tines highly polished and about eight to ten inches long. Yes, here indeed was the perfect head for mounting, and I intended to collect it!

As the buck came up the side, he passed a clearing about sixty yards below me but I fought back this first tempting opportunity to shoot, knowing full well that he must pass closer and perhaps even within sixty feet to the right of me, if he stayed with the run. Melting back quietly under the protective shield of the hemlock, I knelt and waited with bow ready. But as the deer appeared across from me and I finally drew my bow, I forgot about my overhead limitation! The upper bow limb became badly entangled in the branches.

At this slight noise, the buck stopped. He was then looking directly at me. Truly here was a perfect broadside shot at sixty feet, yet I could not even release the arrow! After but a second's hesitation the buck turned, bounding off up towards one of the bench's side feeder trails. Nor was I ever again able to get a chance to release an arrow at that splendid buck!

Later in the day a nice doe came up the same trail but I passed her up in hopes that another buck would chance along. The following day, sure enough, I had my chance and dumped a different buck in the same locale with a spine shot. Knowledge of the game sought put me in the right place for hunting, even though I was in strange country.

I do not, however, expect much action during the better part of the first day when hunting in strange country. Therefore the greater part of this time I move around and check various signs that tell where the deer are feeding and in what pattern they are moving. I check for signs of the kind of feed they are using. If apple trees are to be found, I check such areas thoroughly for signs of deer using them. When most of the apples are still on the tree, I check to see if the ones that have fallen are being eaten. A bare floor covered with ample tracking beneath an apple tree indicates that deer are getting apples on a daily basis, maybe almost as fast as this deer delicacy falls. But if a lot of decaying apples are lying around, I depart right away in search of better hunting places for now the deer's capricious preference for other food has led them elsewhere.

In some instances this suggests too that not many deer, if any at all, are in the whole general area. But when fruit is being eaten and the runs and deer tracks are heavy around the apple trees, I definitely prefer orchard hunting. This deer food is seasonal, however, and not always plentiful in wooded areas, especially if the trees are not being tended.

In orchard hunting I prefer to use a tree stand. If the trees are large enough for the use of such a stand, there is no better place. If the trees are not large enough, I try to locate myself in a tree along some prominent run leading towards the orchard feeding spot.

I get into my stand no later than three o'clock in the afternoon. This allows ample time for settling down before any early evening feeding starts. Too many hunters, I believe, make the mistake of starting for their stand later in the day. If a hunter starts too late, many of the deer will already have worked within close distance of the apple trees; they may be just inside the timber where they will spot the hunter as he comes along. And, after having spotted the hunter and hearing the racket he makes getting into a tree, you can be assured that the deer will not approach that tree anymore the same day for all the apples in whitetail-land!

By getting into your tree watch in plenty of time you may have the pleasant experience of greeting a desirable early-bird deer stepping out into the open, well ahead of his crowd. In many cases this can be a nice buck traveling alone, or maybe just a greedy doe who wants to get at the apples before the rest of her gang gets there.

Just a note of warning. If this early-bird deer happens to be a little fellow, be cautious! Many times such a young deer acts as a sort of scout sent out by the old doe of the group to see if all is clear. If this be the case, this little guy will roam around under the tree and nip an apple or two. Then, after looking around for a while, he will bounce back into the timber. And invariably, if you have not betrayed yourself, the other deer will then step out, one by one, a few minutes later.

One season we hunted a spot where such a curly little fellow did this scouting bit time after time. He would fool around for a quarter of an hour in the orchard, then bounce back into the slashings. When you looked around again after only a few moments, there were the deer, all over the place!

For several days we observed this novel system of deer (or hunter) scouting. Then after one of our party had spotted the rest of the deer just inside the timber with his binoculars, we decided to try spooking this little guy. Allowing him to get under the tree for several minutes, I coughed and off he went. From a distance my companions watched the action through binoculars as the little rascal bounced over into the edge of the timber and checked in with the other deer. Then, after the oldest doe and several others had studied the orchard, they turned and left the area. Nor did they feed on apples that night. We knew, because before we left we shook a fresh stock of apples to the ground, then checked them the next morning.

If you see deer in the woods but do not wish to try for one at the particular time, follow the definite rule of never letting deer know of your presence. Let the deer move away naturally, even if this means a delay for you in traveling to some other point. If a particular deer thus discovers you, he may alarm other deer close by. Many times such other deer will include the buck you want to get. In wildlife, the flight of one or more individuals tends to spook the others. Their flight is a definite communication of danger to the others, hence more will join such headlong flight without hesitation.

There are two appendages on the whitetail, however, which the bowhunter should watch for advance information regarding the deer's next movements. Watch the ears and the tail. Ears pointed forward indicate that the deer has heard a noise that is not trusted. Ears pointed forward also usually mean that the deer has spotted your general location; you must watch your next move carefully.

A wiggling ear means that the deer has detected a noise but that the noise is unidentified and confusing. Wiggling ears therefore also mean that the deer has not yet spotted your general location and that it is waiting for you to make another movement so it can further establish the possibility of danger. That wiggling ear is like the rotating sonar device of a submarine listening, testing, and searching for further noise so source and meaning can be established. If you are downwind at such a time, you can discount any great problem in concealment since only movement will give you away to your quarry. On windy days you will find the deer constantly rotating their ears back and forth as they keep classifying the various noises of the wind, the trees, and the forest. At the first sound that seems unnatural to them they will go on the alert.

Opposite the deer's ears is its famous tail, the "flag." This appendage is a signal flag; it is often used to warn other members of the herd of impending danger. Watch it carefully. It can tell you a lot concerning what will happen in the next few seconds. When not alert or alarmed, the deer will keep its tail down, occasionally twitching it as the deer feeds along. If several deer are feeding together, all is well as long as the tails are down and occasionally twitching. If one of the group should spot some movement, scent some strange odor, or hear a strange noise rest assured that its tail will come up! This is an alarm signal to the others cautioning them to be alert; also, it usually indicates the group's quick departure within seconds. Then all you have for your trouble is a view of the large white tail ruffs as they go bouncing off through the timber.

A sneaking buck is fully aware of the telltale flash of white that his large tail would show if he left it upright. So he tries to keep it tucked down tightly as he slips away through the cover. But try as he may, he cannot seem to prevent an occasional waggle, thus betraying his best efforts to slip away unnoticed.

Often the statement is heard among hunters that the hard-hit deer will keep its tail down. But this does not always hold true. I have shot several bucks with the rifle wherein this did not apply. I also shot one buck with the bow, a case in which he kept his flag flying high as he ran away despite a shaft down through the pelvic bone. But there is something to the statement because as a rule a deer will keep its tail turned down when hit.

One can only conjecture whether this be due to the wound or as a natural effort at concealment.

When several deer are around, you can rely on one being the boss of the bunch. In most cases this is the oldest of the deer and always a doe. If there happens to be a buck in the group, he will not be in charge, though among other animals it is often the case for a male to lead. The whitetail buck, it seems, is far more interested in saving his own skin. He shirks the duty of overseeing the others. Hence he does not step out as the first deer of a group; he never feeds in the very center of a clearing, and he is constantly ready to take flight or sneak away through some cover while the attention of intruders is centered on female members of his group. Employing a female for a decoy or as a means of testing an area before he steps into it is an old trick of the whitetail buck. And more often than not he will circle a clearing while the doe in the group ventures forth less cautiously.

The buck is far more cautious in his manner of movement. His moves are furtive and rather sneaking. Usually he moves along with his head low; if spooked, he will tend to sneak rather than bound openly away. Also, he is less likely than a doe to accept some strange object as natural. Thus he will study such an object intensely for a long time, all the while distrustful and waiting for some telltale movement to warn of danger. Nor will a buck rely on the signals and actions of other deer to confirm that all is well. Instead, he relies on his own hunches and makes a final check for himself.

I have known many cases where in a group of does and younger deer accepted a clearing as being safe and started feeding minutes before a buck stepped into view. The sudden quiet appearance of a buck on such occasions is so surprising and unexpected that you can bet your best bow he is banking on this trick to fool you into believing he is not around. The bowhunter must be ready for such tricks and wait patiently for the buck to make his presence known.

Another trick often employed is for a buck not to appear at all near or through the same entrance from which other deer have come into a clearing. Instead, the buck may circle, then step out directly behind the unsuspecting hunter! The buck may have decided to circle the clearing and to test the wind thoroughly before accepting the locale as safe. This explains why a hunter sometimes hears a snort and the sound of hooves as a deer runs off behind or to the side of him while the hunter's attention was perhaps centered on deer in a clearing to the front.

If a buck has not caught your scent while circling, he may have detected some slight movement on your part and therefore be standing quietly in screening brush watching you intently. At your next move his suspicions are confirmed and he is off! This is why if you are holding out for a buck, it is wise to give a group of deer an extra five minutes or so of quiet motionless surveillance while at the same time remaining alert to the possibility of a buck stepping out near you.

During the early part of the archery season, I have found that bucks prefer to travel alone or in pairs. Since rutting season then has not usually started, they prefer the company of their own sex. A great number of bucks travel and feed alone. Perhaps this is why they are far more cautious in their manner of feeding, in some cases starting to feed along the very edge of a clearing but never actually wandering into the center of it at all. Evidently they well know the advantage of staying close to the edge of screening timber or brush where one or two jumps will take them out of view.

I have often had a buck stop at the edge of a clearing where good feed was available, stand there for minutes testing the wind, then turn and disappear without ever eating a mouthful. Some stray scent may have reached the deer's nostrils, or maybe the buck's natural wariness persuaded him to return to cover. Or, maybe he just was following a vague instinctive hunch against risking his neck in a locale not recently explored by does. But in any case, the direction and movement of air currents in the hunter's locale are very important.

In all mountainous terrain, for example, there is a definite and natural pattern of air movement peculiar to morning and evening periods. Such thermal movements are created by the rising and setting of the sun. As the sun rises in the morning the air is warmed and rises towards the tops of ridges, thus creating an upward flow of air along side hills from their bottoms to their tops. As the sun sets in the evening, cool air flows from the top to the bottom of the side hills.

This reversal in air movement takes place every morning and evening during normal fair calm weather. To remember this for your future hunting just think of the air following the sun: it rises up the side hill in the morning with the sunrise and likewise goes down the side hill in the evening as the sun goes down; or hunt high and look down in the early morning and hunt low and look up in the evening.

The following tactics for successful deer stands in sidehill hunting therefore evolve. Stay below your deer in the evening if they are coming down; stay above your deer in the morning if they are going up. If you post yourself at the top of a ridge in order to be adjacent to clearings (feeding areas) for evening hunting, deer coming up may scent you easily and swing around your stand. In such a hunting situation it is best to be posted on the far side of the clearings and away from the edge of the ridge or hill to minimize possibilities of the game scenting you. Likewise, stay away from the bottom of a ridge if you wish to intercept deer bound for ridgetops after feeding in the bottoms in the morning. If these deer must ascend the ridge on their way to their bedding grounds you are likely to do better if posted above the deer where you can face the upward flow of air along the sidehill, thus being actually downwind of deer below you.

Ignorant of this daily reversal in the flow of air, many a bowhunter has taken a post on a good run and remained there for hours without seeing any deer and probably not realizing that deer came near but scented him and made a wide detour around his position to work on up the sidehill without the hunter's knowledge. The evening hunter may have experienced similar reactions of deer bound down the sidehills to early feeding spots along the bottoms. Having taken a watch at the top of some good run, he was scented by the deer headed past him. By making short detours circling the hunter, the deer could slip past and go on down without being sighted.

Well back in the bottoms and away from ridge sides, air in the mornings has a tendency to rise straight upwards instead of in the up and down flow patterns just referred to. Accordingly, I pick a stand in such an area well back from a ridge side, thus being reasonably set to intercept deer bound for higher bedding grounds.

Late evenings, when I post with the intention of intercepting deer traveling towards lower feeding areas, I pick a spot at the far side of areas adjacent to the top of the sidehill from which I am expecting deer. Again, I thus try to stay downwind of expected game by placing myself where there is the least possibility of air flowing from me towards the deer.

If you disregard this daily pattern of air reversal and place yourself in the wrong spot, all you are likely to get for your trouble is the sound of a short snort of alarm as some old doe tells every other deer in the neighborhood of your presence. For an encore maybe you'll hear the sound of running hooves as the deer circle around you well out of sight and out of shooting range.

There is, however, a brief period preceding the morning air movement cycle during which a complete calm may exist on a windless day. This calm occurs just between dawn and sunrise, before the first rays of the rising sun activate the daily air currents. Also, in the evening this calm period may follow the setting of the sun and last until dusk. The calm should set in about when the last rays of the setting sun have disappeared for the day. When shooting is legal during these periods of motionless air there is less chance of deer scenting you, a factor well in your favor. The whitetail, of course, is doubly cautious during these periods; he is always a wily master analyst of air and wind currents.

My records, nevertheless, indicate that the morning calm periods are best for hunting; in the evening calm periods deer are doubly cautious in approaching open areas. The same records also suggest that the feeding habits of game may be influenced by certain phases of the moon.

Opinions concerning the influence of the moon on feeding habits of game are diverse. Some hunters agree there is some lunar influence but others scoff at it as a significant factor. I believe that every hunter should determine for himself from his own experience and notes whether or not such influences are worthy as planning references for future hunting trips.

While hunting with both rifle and bow, I have made a careful study over a period of fifteen or more years regarding the moon's effect on the feeding habits of game. Based on my personal experiences and observations I am inclined to believe that the feeding activity of both cottontail rabbits and whitetailed deer is affected by the various periods of the lunar cycle.

Periods of full moon mean curtailed feeding activities of deer in early pre-dusk as well as late morning hours. During the last quarters of the old moon and the first quarters of the new moon there is much feeding activity in pre-dusk and post-dawn hours. The rising of the moon also seems to signal a start of feeding periods and commencement of movement of game to feeding grounds.

Take time to observe and check on this during your next hunting season. In periods when the moon rises during daylight hours and can be seen in the late afternoon sky, I believe you will find more deer activity as the whitetails move towards their feeding grounds; there will also be noticeably less game movement during the days when the moon rises late or after dark.

Keep in mind that deer usually move a good distance from their bedding grounds. Therefore it should be easiest to study or check up on game movements at points near the start of such journeys.

I have noticed that pre-storm hunting is also good, especially when you are lucky enough to find deer filling up on extra feed for a lay-over or fast during the stormy-weather period. At such times they are likely to ignore their normal habit of bedding down during midday and feed throughout the day instead.

Whitetail normally react to stormy weather by seeking shelter from the wind and the elements and by staying put until the storm has passed. At the height of the storm deer will usually be found huddled on the sheltered side of a ledge or ridge where they are protected from wind and driving rain or snow. If you are hunting at such times, there is very little chance of the deer moving past you.

9

Methods of Hunting -- Records of Hits

TREE hunting is my choice as the most effective way of hunting whitetail deer with the bow. It affords ideal concealment for the hunter, in most cases not revealing any of his movements to the deer. It usually allows close-range shots, and an excellent opportunity for vital hits such as through spine or neck shots or heart and lung shots delivered with maximum cast and power of the bow. In most cases the shots will be within forty yards, sometimes directly under the tree at twenty feet. Often the well placed shot from a tree stand will pass completely through the deer and lodge in the ground. The deadly spine shot is most effective from a tree position, and it will definitely anchor your deer for keeps.

Whether it be a tree stand, or a ledge overlooking some bench or the top of a side ridge, stay *above* your deer whenever possible. For some unexplainable reason, the whitetail does not tend to look up as he does to the front, rear, or sides. In my hunting, I have tried to apply tactics similar to those I have used successfully in rifle hunting, keeping to terrain above the deer and actually following them as they moved along a side ridge. I have downed several bucks in this manner without first alarming them in any way.

I never try to shoot a deer while it is looking in my direction for my movement in raising the bow and releasing the arrow would be spotted instantly by the deer. In such attempts the deer will invariably bolt or "jump the arrow." It is far better to wait for an opportunity to shoot when the deer is looking the other way, or when it is bending over to nip some browse.

When a tree stand is not possible, a watch on the ground can be inaugurated with almost as good chances for shooting.

But stand where a tree trunk or rock will help break your outline. This also helps screen the movements necessary in releasing your arrow.

Experience has taught me that too much concealment has disadvantages. Freedom of movement for a shot is often hampered in thick concealment. I prefer a stand in fairly open cover and rely on trying to remain motionless as a means of offsetting lack of cover. When you choose a stand, keep in mind the amount of room necessary for handling your bow.

Open-field hunting is a tough task for the bowhunter. Here stalking is practically impossible; to assume a stand without cover is just about as worthless an undertaking. I have found one method of open-field hunting to yield a fair degree of success but do not advise it unless you are hunting on restricted land. Using this method, lying prone in grass about twelve-inches high at the very center of a field in which deer were feeding early in the evening, I had deer come within thirty yards of me. But should you try this method, be prepared for some very unorthodox shots. Your movements have to be well planned and your exact shot procedure decided upon well before moving a finger. For when you start moving, you can count on the fact that the deer will spot you immediately. Therefore, your movements from prone to a sitting shooting position must be combined in one smooth and swift maneuver. Ordinarily you can hope for only a running shot, at best.

In stalking or sneak hunting with the bow, the same rules apply as to the rifle hunter. Walk one step, stop and look for several minutes, then take another step, etc. Be mindful of the air currents; always work *into* the wind. Never forget to look *behind* you as well as to the front and the sides. Do not worry about achieving utmost stealth in movement, for deer too make a certain amount of noise as they move. Confine the noise you make to about the maximum you might expect would be made by a deer. The most important thing to keep in mind, really, is that if the deer spots you first, your shooting will be at long range and your target will be flashing away at a very fast pace.

Driving deer can be a productive hunting method for the bowhunter as well as the rifleman. Here again thorough knowledge of the country is necessary for good results. Watchers must be placed properly and the drivers must push the deer along one of their natural routes and directions of travel. Drivers must proceed slowly and quietly so that the deer will drift along ahead without being "spooked" into full flight. If all goes well, the watchers will most often get standing or walking shots. Groups I have hunted with have used this hunting system very effectively, and taken some nice deer.

Terrain is very important when the driving hunting method is used. A natural pattern of deer movement exists which seem to be governed both by geography and the food supply. Deer driven along a side hill or ridge will usually circle the point, then cut back on the opposite side. Or, they may cross, or leave the ridge at a saddle or ravine. Sometimes a few deer will break and go over the ridge's top. In most cases though, where the drive is properly slow and silent, this will not happen. When the drive is performed correctly, the deer are not being pushed into full flight but instead are being moved along with little or no alarm, convinced evidently that they are eluding the drivers.

Every ridge has its favorite heavily-used, deer crossing, travel routes. These should always be duly invested with watchers. In most cases, the deer will ghost along slowly ahead of the drivers, following their natural path of travel, even stopping at times to mill around or feed no more than one hundred yards ahead of the careful oncoming drivers.

The hunters on watch can expect deer driven carefully to move very naturally. They will move quite differently from the wild flight of whitetails agitated in some of the shouting and crashing drives employed by rifle hunters. The former method is not only preferable but *necessary* to allow shots at ranges proper for the bowhunter. He must try for the close shot on a slowly moving target whenever possible.

Sometimes draws or ravines offer the possibility of "funneling" deer through a narrow section of heavy cover. Deer will often accept this kind of a route in preference to one in which their emergency escape route would require them to break up over the sides of a seemingly blocked ravine in open timber. And they will accept it easiest if being driven silently.

Flatland and swampy areas are the hardest terrain in which to drive deer. In this kind of country the cover and escape routes are many. From a deer's point of view, each one is as easy to follow as the other. Upon carefully examining such country, you will find a maze of feeder and travel runs going in every direction. This terrain is not at all comparable to that having side ridges and benches, where the trails are less numerous but better defined. So for flatland and swamp hunting terrain the watchers should be posted at spots where the trails lead in and out of the heaviest thicket. Bear in mind that the whitetail will choose the best screened escape routes whenever possible. It follows that in such country, the drivers must be doubly alert for deer "cutting back" or circling behind them. This is another common trait of the whitetail. The alert but silent driver, nevertheless, stands a good chance of spotting any deer which attempt this maneuver.

One of my hunting companions, an ardent hunter who has brought down his share of whitetails with the bow, has a special admonition he always passes along to the budding bowhunters he meets. He warns them against "over-sweating" a deer up to close range, basing his advice on knowledge of the harmful tensions which too often afflict bowhunters at critical times. He advises them to take their shot at a deer at the first opportunity presented within range instead of passing up such chances in hopes of later but closer shots. His reasoning merits thought.

Usually, when a deer is spotted out of range, tension starts to build up within the hunter as he waits and "sweats out" the deer, slowly working its way closer. The first possible shot may be at forty yards, open, and the deer standing. But too often the hunter concludes that the deer is still working in his direction. He will get a better shot, he thinks. So he passes up that first possible shot in the expectation of a closer one. As he continues to wait and the deer works closer, the hunter's nerves get tighter and his mouth goes dry. He freezes with bow in a ready position, arrow nocked and ready for quick draw and release. The closer the deer gets, the longer the hunter waits; the longer the "sweating" period, the greater the nervous tension! When the deer finally gets into close-range position where a "guzzy" shot should be almost anticlimactic, the hunter is such a bundle of nerves the result is the unbelievable miss!

A common curse in this predicament is unconsciously pinching the nock while one is in the throes of trying to be a real wooden Indian. Other hunters will overdraw in this state of tightly corked up emotion. And most such close-range shots go high, for in very few cases does the bowhunter ever then seem to shoot low. Flinching, too, is almost inevitable; in fact, practically uncontrollable in such situations.

By applying the theory of taking your shot at a deer when the first opportunity presents itself within proper range, you eliminate most of these problems. First, you have not as yet developed any tension, since after all you only spotted the deer a minute or so ago. Thus you are still quite relaxed for the shot.

Your shooting now will be smoother and minus that built-up "bundle of nerves" effect.

Secondly, the average bowhunter is usually more accurate at about forty yards than he is at extremely close ranges. On the longer shots he aims and releases with more concentration. The close-shot opportunity on the other hand implies that he can't miss. So less time is taken in holding tightly. In fact, in most close-shot cases the shooter merely shoots for the body and this spells MISS more times than not!

Thirdly, the game animal is less likely to become aware of the hunter at a forty-yard range than at twenty. This means a more stable target at the former yardage, one that will remain in one given spot long enough to allow a well-aimed hit. As the game gets closer to the hunter it becomes increasingly aware of danger. Soon the deer becomes a nervous and very alert target, one skittish and ready to burst into flight at the flick of the hunter's eyelid.

Take your pick of targets, the unsuspecting buck at about forty yards as he stands looking back over his shoulder, or a brown blurred shape spinning away at twenty yards. The first deer will probably never see you make your draw. The second one will; that's why he's rarely bagged.

Yet another aspect of aiming requires advice. This concerns the moment when you find the shaft lined up and ready for release. *Don't hesitate!* Loose your arrow the moment your hold feels right. In the instant you doubt your hold, you defeat your instinctive judgment. That first feeling of being on target is more likely to augur a good hit than the later one to which some little adjustment was added through doubt. And if you make such little prolonged aiming adjustments, they constitute an open-faced admission that you were guessing, ignoring all the natural instinctive feelings about aim that required so many days of practice time to develop.

The experienced bowhunter does not release an arrow without sensing its accuracy before it hits the target. The moment it leaves the bow you should know if it is going to be "in the money" or not. When a good hit comes as a surprise to the shooter, it is evidence that he has not yet developed enough skill with his weapon. Confidence is one of the satisfying results of constant practice; it cannot be purchased with the bow, but it *will grow* with practice. And practice such as obtained through hunting helps too.

No doubt hunting is the best of all teachers. With twenty-five years of hunting under my belt, I still learn something new about deer each year. But without some of this experience, I am sure I would not have tagged many a buck. The point is that no two big-game animals will very often react to the hunter or the hunting situation in the same way. So the more varied experience you acquire, the better off you are. Consider, for example, some of the variations evident in the following summaries of deer taken.

My first buck, killed from a tree stand, was taken through a shot at a fifty-foot range and on a downward angle of about forty-five degrees from a fifty-five pound bow employing twenty-eight inch shafts tipped with Hilbre hunting heads. As the buck came along he spotted me in the low branch, then stopped in his tracks. Not able to draw while he watched me, I realized that my shot would have to be made as he turned to run away. Watching him closely, I saw his nervousness betray his intentions. Thus I was able to anticipate his initial turning leap, assuming he would run back in the direction from which he had just come, and where he knew all had been safe midst the protective timber.

As he spun I made a fast draw and released the shaft, holding for his front shoulder. In the time it took my arrow to travel that fifty feet he had moved quite a bit. Thus the hit was down through the rump and smashing through the pelvic bone. The impact of the arrow drove his hind-quarters down towards the ground in a straddling position, but recovering, he took off at a full run towards the top of the ridge, then dropped dead. He had run a distance of one hundred and fifty yards along the first bench, where he fell. With the femoral artery between the hind legs completely severed, hemorrhage had been completed in that distance. Before pursuing him, I allowed fifteen minutes to elapse.

My second proved to be a running shot on a steep ledge at a distance of forty yards. Again I used the fifty-five pound bow with twenty-eight inch arrows tipped with Hilbre hunting points. Ready for him at a spot where he had to turn in running along the trail, I released my arrow just ahead of his chest. The hit was high on the front shoulder with the shaft glancing along the top of the shoulder blade and lodging in the center of a vertebrae but at the same time cutting the spinal cord. The buck reared, then toppled backwards to the base of the ledge, pinned down with a broken back. A quick but well-placed heart shot than finished him within minutes.

In this instance I had been waiting for the approach of the first doe in a group of deer that I had earlier spotted on the bench below me; starting up the ledge trail they had alerted me early. While I waited motionless with bow in ready position, the lead doe came into view and paused. Because she then glanced down over the ledge, I followed her eyes, thus spotting the buck below. When he turned and started up the ledge to join her, the doe turned and went back down the trail out of sight. Bucks can be around at the most unpredictable places!

A third buck entailed a shot of fifty yards on a rainy, foggy morning in very poor light. With only a body silhouette for a target, I loosed my arrow while holding for his front shoulder. Just at the release, the buck stepped forward and the hit occurred dead center of the hind leg, about eight-inches low. The arrow completely penetrated both hams, its head piercing the skin on the deer's far side. This time I was shooting a fifty-pound bow and using twenty-eight inch shafts tipped with Hill hunting heads and the shot was made through screening brush. I ran into the open immediately to see which way the buck ran, then followed him at once.

Rain swiftly obliterated all blood sign. This, coupled with the prevailing poor light, made it impossible to see tracks. But after running eighty yards to the lower corner of the foggy clearing, the deer threw the shaft. Then it turned, ran another twenty yards and fell, finished within two minutes. The arrow had severed the femoral artery of both hind legs.

During a more recent hunt, one member of our group hit a one-hundred-pound doe in the rear and slightly to the left of the anus opening. He was shooting a fifty-pound bow with twenty-eight-inch shafts tipped with Hilbre hunting tips. This shot was made at a distance of about forty yards, and the arrow penetrated slightly over four inches. The deer ran about fifty yards and fell. Before dying, it several times attempted to turn and bite the shaft. In this case the arrowhead had barely cut the femoral artery. This is a case wherein the deer went down within sight of the hunter.

On another hunt, one of my companions made a paunch hit on a seventy-five pound doe. He used a fifty-pound bow with twenty-seven-inch shafts tipped with Hilbre heads. The shot occurred at about fifty yards as the deer jumped from its bed in a heavy thicket. This doe then ran about one hundred and fifty yards and fell with twenty inches of the shaft imbedded. This, of course, kept cutting while the deer ran. The hunter immediately followed the deer and struck it with a second arrow as it tried to get up. All was over within five minutes.

A season not long ago this same hunter placed an arrow in the neck of a larger (hundred and twenty-pound) doe at a distance of forty yards. Using the same equipment as before, his arrow passed completely through the deer's neck, severing the carotid or jugular artery. This deer fell within sixty yards of the location at which it received the arrow. It was therefore still within sight of the hunter. Death was almost simultaneous with its fall.

On another hunting trip one member of our party placed an arrow in the liver of a very large doe while standing post as a watcher during a silent drive. He was shooting a fifty-pound bow and using twenty-eight-inch shafts tipped with Bear razorheads. Penetration was about twelve inches. Before falling dead, the deer ran for one hundred and fifty yards. This deer was followed, after the hunter had waited ten minutes. It was a beauty, weighing out to one hundred and forty pounds field dressed.

Some other case summaries follow which have been taken from the records of an experienced hunting companion. Deer weights are given as field dressed, and unless otherwise stated, the equipment used was a sixty-pound bow casting twenty-eight-inch arrows with Hill heads.

Deer No. 1, a buck weighing seventy pounds, was shot with a fifty-three-pound bow casting twenty-eight-inch shafts with Ben Pearson heads. During a silent drive this running deer was hit at an extremely close range, only three yards, by a hunter posted on watch. The arrow penetrated the lungs to a depth of twelve inches. The deer fell dead after running for one hundred and fifteen yards. A waiting period of twenty minutes elapsed before the hunter followed the deer.

Deer No. 2, a doe weighing one hundred and twenty pounds, was shot with the same weight bow as in the preceding case, but when twenty-eight-inch arrows tipped with Bear razorheads were in use. The deer was hit in the paunch at forty-two yards, the arrow passing completely through the deer. The deer ran one hundred and fifty yards before falling. A waiting period of one and one-half hours elapsed before the hunter followed the deer.

Deer No. 3, a buck weighing seventy pounds, was shot with the fifty-three pound bow casting twenty-eight-inch arrows tipped with Howard Hill heads. It was hit at thirty yards and fell in its tracks with a broken spine.

Deer No. 4, a buck weighing one hundred and twenty-five pounds, was shot at thirty-five yards, the arrow passing through the heart and then entirely through the deer. Before falling dead the deer traveled ninety yards, however weather and circumstances intervened to prevent pursuit of this deer at that time. It was not found therefore until early the next morning.

Deer No. 5, a buck weighing eighty-five pounds, was shot with the fifty-three pound bow. This was a lung hit made at twenty-five yards; penetration was in as far as the arrow's fletching. The deer fell dead after running seventy yards. Before following this deer, however, the hunter waited twenty minutes.

Deer No. 6, a doe weighing one hundred pounds, was shot with the same bow. It was hit at sixty yards, the arrow breaking a hind leg. Immediately after the hit this deer was tracked for a prolonged time (five hours) during which it traveled about one and one-half miles. Finally, weakened and cornered, it was killed with a second shot.

Deer No. 7, a buck weighing one hundred and twenty-five pounds, was shot with the same kind of arrow (Hill) but cast by a seventy-five-pound bow. This was a lung hit at thirty yards with the arrow penetrating in to the fletching. The deer ran for one hundred and twenty-five yards before falling dead. A waiting period of half an hour elapsed before the hunter began tracking the deer. This shot was made from a tree during a stalking hunt.

Deer No. 8, a buck weighing one hundred and ten pounds, was hit in the heart at forty yards. The arrow passed completely through the deer which, nevertheless, ran one hundred and twenty-five yards before falling dead. A waiting time of one hour passed before the hunter followed the deer.

Deer No. 9, a buck weighing only ninety-five pounds, was hit in the paunch while bounding along at a twenty-five-yard range. This deer ran half a mile, then bedded. The hunter followed it immediately, pushing it a distance of over one mile. After four hours of tracking and stalking, it was then killed with another shot. The first arrow had penetrated in as far as the fletching.

Deer No. 10, a doe weighing one hundred and fifty pounds, was shot from a tree stand. The hit occurred in the lungs at a range of twelve yards. Although the arrow penetrated as far as its fletching, this deer ran for one hundred and fifty yards before falling dead. The hunter allowed one and one-half hours to elapse before following the deer.

Deer No. 11, a doe weighing ninety-five pounds, was hit in the spine at forty-five yards and fell in its tracks but a second arrow to the heart was required to kill it. The chance for taking this deer came while the hunter was posted on a cross-trail.

The particular bowhunter to whom the preceding eleven cases are ascribed is a highly competent hunter. His knowledge of deer, skill in shooting, and ability to track are highly developed. He follows a firm rule regarding the amount of time which he feels should elapse before a hunter follows a hit deer. This is no less than twenty minutes if the deer is believed to have sustained a good hit, or no less than one hour if the hit is regarded doubtful or a poor one. But the length of the waiting time, if any, that should elapse before a hunter undertakes to follow his wounded deer is much discussed. Like other questions in hunting, it has its two sides. My own view on this differs from that held by many other experienced bowhunters.

I contend that if the hit is vital and the deer is bleeding badly internally, the hunter should follow the deer immediately without any attendant fear of thus lessening his chances of recovering it. My "right after the deer" or "hot pursuit" philosophy considers weather and forest conditions, factors often not sufficiently considered. For example, much bowhunting takes place in dry forest. In this environment, tracking blood trails can be very difficult since some of the usual tracking aids, a deer's hoof prints, for example, are hard to distinguish on dry, leafy forest floors. Hence, by following your deer right after the hit, the time spent in finding the deer is apt to be much shorter. Blood sign, if any, should be fresher and easier to see. Even the deer's tracks should prove easier to find midst tree leaves, etc., especially with the deer's location when hit still very fresh in mind.

Then, too, I also believe that if a deer is hit well enough to induce profuse internal bleeding, it will be able to run only a certain limited distance before it must collapse from weakness and shock through blood loss. It seems to me this distance should not vary so greatly regardless of whether the deer is followed immediately or later on. So there would seem to be no good reason for waiting any specific time period before undertaking the trailing. Therefore, I favor immediate tracking.

Incidentally, in many cases, by following a wounded deer right away you may be able to hear some of its struggles after it has fallen. Needless to say, if this should happen it would tend to greatly speed your locating the deer. Notice, too, that this possible advantage almost always is denied those who choose to wait some period of time instead of immediate tracking.

Weather conditions, terrain, hunter pressure, etc., exert a strong influence on the question of whether or not a particular wounded deer can be recovered quickly. If the hit is a non-vital one and the quantity of blood lost not great, this theory of following the deer at once still proves sound if carried out thoughtfully. Keep in mind that a deer wounded in such a moderate degree will still continue to weaken through continued movement. This movement will keep the wound actively bleeding and there will usually be continuous blood loss. On the other hand if the wounded animal is permitted to bed and rest, it may conserve its strength for another escape effort. In some cases its wound may stop bleeding entirely through coagulation, especially if it does not have to greatly exert itself. I contend that there are many cases involving non-vital hits, such as where the arrow has penetrated the stomach or intestinal tract, in which wound damage is more effectively compounded by keeping the deer moving rather than by giving it a chance to rest. The cutting and sawing action of the broadhead while lodged in such a deer will be constant as the animal walks or runs and this damage should not be underestimated. But if a wounded deer beds and is quiet, the opposite will result. Each additional vein which can be cut by the deer's movement will result in more blood loss and thus eventually the deer must stop permanently.

Since the bowhunter should always seek to get within range for a second killing shot, the hunter will be aided considerably in tracking by the additional blood loss incurred as the deer is forced to push on. Through reading such a blood trail properly you can tell whether you are doing right or not in applying the "right-after-the-deer" philosophy. Any hit made in some part of the body where arteries or veins are small means loss of only a small volume of blood. However, by pushing deer in such cases, the bleeding will be aggravated. Were such a deer allowed to bed down, chances are that coagulation might close the wound and stop hemorrhaging. Then the deer could conserve its strength and recover enough to later travel very great distances, possibly never to be found.

Bright red blood, of course, indicates an artery hit. Dark red blood indicates veinous hits, possibly a hit in the liver. If the blood shows any green or yellowish cast, it usually means a hit in the paunch with either stomach or intestinal contents being mixed in the blood.

No doubt many won't agree with this theory of "hot pursuit," swearing by some preliminary waiting period instead. This is fair enough, though the hunter should not follow traditional procedures blindly nor without good reason or trial to see for himself. Concerning my own experiments, details are included in Chapter 12, Blood Volume and Shock, and there provide, I believe, a frame of reference against which my "right-after-the-deer" concept may be more sharply focused.

10

Misses on Whitetails With the Bow

THOUGH advantageous in bowhunting for maximum point-blank range and adequate penetration of game, a bow of heavy poundage will limit the shooter's practice sessions. Some archers seem to think that a few long periods of constant shooting constitutes better conditioning than a greater number of shorter periods. But prolonged practice sessions with heavy equipment work to the detriment of good conditioning, I think, and bring about physical exhaustion which compounds errors.

Very few bowhunters can shoot around a twenty-eight target field course with a heavy hunting bow of fifty-pounds-plus draw without tiring severely. Bear in mind that this involves the shooting of one hundred and twelve arrows, yet the bowhunter enjoying a very good day's hunting may fire but six arrows. By unnecessarily long practice sessions, therefore, the archer subjects himself to much physical exertion which can prove more harmful than beneficial to shooting skill.

The sensible way to practice between seasons and to stay in condition is to limit your shooting to short daily periods, shooting no more than fifty arrows. This will avoid undue fatigue, keep the shooter loose and his eye sharp. This, of course, will not apply to the archer who is shooting a light bow in such practice periods. On the other hand the light bow in practice work will do little to ready the archer for practical hunting. It merely defers the problem of transition to heavier tackle until just prior to the hunting season.

The bowhunter will benefit most by using targets which resemble at all times the outline or sighting picture of the animal he intends to hunt. Targets with a conventional field face or the hunter face are of negligible value in helping the bowhunter to develop his ability to pick a proper aiming spot on a game animal.

Whether the target be a paper-traced outline of the animal or a cardboard-cutout body profile, or a commercial big-game target face, the important thing is to cultivate selection and skill with respect to hitting a specific point in practice. I would rather shoot at a vertically suspended burlap bag filled with straw than any field-type target face. The reason for this is because such a target presents no special pimple or other tempting aiming spot for placing the arrow. Instead it requires the shooter to visualize and place his arrow on a self-selected aiming spot. This is a realistic condition that will apply in connection with bagging any big-game animal the bowhunter will hunt. Unfortunately, many archers find themselves at a loss to pick such an imaginary aiming spot and also lacking in ability to group several arrows accurately and consistently in a self-chosen target area. Thus many misses are also encountered when they go hunting.

The bowhunter who can pick a spot on a burlap bag target at various distances then angle his arrows consistently to his aiming points will have no difficulty in placing his arrow whenever the opportunity is offered on game anatomy, providing, of course, the game target is in proper range. Also, if he uses broadheads in his practice shooting, he avoids the problems which frequently attend the transition from use of target to field or hunting heads with their differing points of impact.

Yet all bowhunters will miss! This failing is not restricted to the novice or beginner, but is seen even among the most skilled. In a great number of cases the main contributing factor is some fault of the hunter, although it sometimes can be fairly traced to some movement of the quarry or other outside factor. But regardless of how it happens, the bowhunter has the obligation of making sure that if he misses game, his miss will be a clean one. This means that he must thoroughly check the action area to verify whether or not he actually missed or whether he might have slightly wounded a deer. The time lost in doing this is not really wasted by hunters, for it is quite educational in every respect. By analyzing the shot, finding your arrow, checking it back from the target to your shooting point, etc., you will gain a different perspective than the one you find through only looking over the shaft in shooting. Usually thought of as uninstructive by the average archer, miss analysis on the contrary can improve one's ability to detect faults, for a lot of time and searching indeed can be involved in looking for a wayward shaft!

When the miss is due to some fault of the hunter, it is sometimes hard to deduct just what was done wrong to throw the shot off. But, in most cases careful reflection will usually give you the needed clue.

The most common errors made when hunting usually involve the arrow release. Of these, flinching or plucking are the most common, with pinching the nock being next in line. Flinching is the fault in shooting which occurs whenever an archer or rifle shooter fails to subordinate his wish to get off a shoot or to release an arrow to his efforts in first achieving proper aim. Through carelessness in the arrow release, an archer may be guilty of plucking; that is, he may flip or pluck his drawing hand quickly away from his face, sometimes almost at right angles to the arrow's intented flight as he releases it, and perhaps with subconscious effort to get his fingers out of the way of the bowstring. And pinching means clutching the arrow too tightly between the fingers of the drawing hand during the draw. A release in which the bow arm is dropped too soon so that the archer can try to see his arrow hit will throw the shot low. This I can personally vouch for.

Partial draw as well as overdrawing will affect the flight of your arrow. Failing to pick a specific target spot on the deer is a common problem among bowhunters. Too many of them instead shoot for the entire body or a very general portion of same. The cause, of course, is lack of concentration. The result everytime is a wild shot.

To the instinctive archer, misjudging distance is the same bug-a-boo as a poor estimate of range is to the rifleman. The archer who habitually draws to a high anchor point, such as the cheekbone, and who does not use some form of aiming device or bowsight is often referred to as an "instinctive archer," despite the fact that it is much practice rather than natural instinct that affects his scoring the most. The archer, however, has less margin for error; whereas the rifle hunter may miss his aiming point but still get a hit, the bowhunter usually will miss completely.

Unfortunately, both rifle hunters and bowhunters sometimes hit game, but the game goes unrecovered. Then the game animal likely dies later, wasting away in the forest. But not always is this traceable to carelessness by the hunter. Conditions sometimes make it plainly impossible for him to locate wounded game.

This is bound to happen in hunting, though the amount of game loss can be lessened through a hunter's restraint and by his waiting for a sure shot rather than attempting a chance opportunity at a poor target.

Some sincere and dedicated hunters have actually hit and wounded deer in bowhunting but assumed a miss; many have made non-vital hits without any knowledge whatsoever of having done so. It is impossible to say just how many of these deer survive, how long they survive, or how many must die well before their natural time. I am prone to conjecture that such deer hit with a hunting arrow stand a better chance for survival than those hit with the high-power rifle bullet.

We usually are agreed that the initial shock inflicted by a hunting arrow at best is negligent; deer thus wounded may be left in far better physical condition to counteract the wound. With the arrow, extensive amounts of tissue destruction do not occur in comparison with the rifle bullet, which mushrooms. Since the channel of the arrow wound is also restricted to passage of the head and the shaft diameter, self-healing of arrow wounds among deer may be extensive.

There are many cases in the files of the various state game departments which concern deer found to contain imbedded heads of hunting arrows, discovered in dressing out the venison. Often, these heads are completely encased in healthy tissue. To all appearances, these deer were not adversely nor permanently affected by such injuries. Usually these cases have come to light in deer shot by rifle hunters who, when they saw how the broadheads were encased without infection, were bound to reflect that if it had been a rifle-bullet wound involved rather than an arrow wound, the deer would likely not have survived.

I received a call one day from a sportsman friend of mine who manages a butcher shop. A great guy at heart, he offers free venison butchering for all his regular customers. Now he was rendering a doe carcass, one which had been shot during the special antlerless season.

In sawing down through the center of the backbone to separate the two sides of the carcass, he heard a rasping sound as his saw cut through the vertebrae. Stopping to check for possible bullet fragments, he discovered a broadhead firmly lodged between two vertebrae. He then called me, telling of his discovery. By the time I got there he had carefully cut out the portion in which the arrowhead was lodged but he left enough meat around it to show surrounding tissue and bone.

We believe this deer had been earlier shot by some bowhunter during that same year's archery season which started in the first week of October. That season preceded the regular deer hunting season and the later special one-day antlerless season in which the deer was finally taken, December seventeenth, by some two and one-half months.

The bowhunter responsible for the arrow wound had made a high hit far to the back. His arrow passed through half of the deer and penetrated a little better than three inches beyond the far side of the backbone. The arrowhead was lodged tightly between two vertebrae, its point barely breaking through the skin on the opposite side.

A growth of healthy scar tissue had started to form immediately around the broadhead. There was little if any drainage noticeable at the point where the arrow extruded through the skin. A veterinarian pronounced the meat entirely edible, there being no contrary indication of any kind.

It is unlikely that this wound left any or enough blood trail to have been useful in following the deer. Nor was there any appreciable amount of internal bleeding. There are few blood vessels in the part of the deer affected. Also, it is unlikely that this injury handicapped the deer's travel. Likely the hunter was ignorant of the wound. All considered, this is typical of those cases where the bowhunter believes he may have hit the deer but lost it in the absence of any trail.

Had it been a rifle bullet rather than an arrow, the deer would likely have fallen and been recovered. The bullet's shocking power would probably have broken this deer's back. However, I can't help but think of this case and how the arrow wound healed every time I hear statements about deer running around in the woods with arrows sticking from them which caused the deer to wither away to a painful death.

11

Whitetail Anatomy, Picking Your Spot

PLACING your arrow in any portion of the chest cavity, that part of the deer covered by the rib cage, usually will count as a vital hit. Two very vital organs, the lungs and the heart, are here. These organs are vulnerable to profuse bleeding if hit by a hunting arrow. Here, therefore, is a summary of some hits, considered in the order of their usual effectiveness.

Lung Hits

This is one of the most effective hits for the bowhunter and it involves the largest target areas. This also is the case, of course, with all big game. If the bowhunter will take the time to examine the lungs closely when he field-dresses his deer, he will find they have a spongy texture, containing countless tiny blood vessels. Supplied by a network of arteries and thousands of small blood vessels, the deer's blood supply is constantly circulated into and out of these two bellow-like organs. Oxygen taken from the air is added to the blood through the tiny cellular sponges; once charged with oxygen, the blood is then pumped to all parts of the body along the arterial route. Returned through the veinous system, the blood is again purified by fresh oxygen and sent on its way, the cycle being continuous with each breath of the animal.

A broadhead arrow passing into or through a lung is definite assurance that the deer or other big-game animal will fall within a relatively short distance. If a large artery is cut, death may be instantaneous in some cases. Usually the animal will travel until its lungs have filled through bleeding, eventually drowning. A deer or other big-game animal that has run a considerable distance *before* an arrow strikes him may have become exhausted, then a lung hit could cause the animal to fall instantly. Overheated blood warms the air in the lungs but a sudden hole created, as when a shaft passes completely through the deer, allows cooler outer air to enter the lungs. This circumstance can induce lung collapse, asphyxiation, and quick death. The trail left by a big-game animal hit in the lungs is frothy in pattern, pinkish-red in color, and notably sprayed to the sides of the animal's tracks because of the bellow-like action of the lungs. The hunter can usually expect to recover a deer hit this way within one hundred to one hundred and fifty yards.

Under some conditions it is possible that the hunter may actually hear sounds which will identify the deer as wounded. The bowhunter is not crowded while he is hunting; often, he is the only hunter in his particular area and if it is not too windy his hearing range may be surprisingly increased in the natural quiet of the forest.

The noises and sounds made by wounded game offer a clue to the hunter concerning many things: location of the game, its direction of travel, its travel abilities and, of greatest importance, the place where it may be foundering. If the forest is dry, and the wind is not too strong when the hunter listens, such unusual noises can be heard for some distance. The lung-hit deer will not always run away in wild flight, especially if the deer has not spotted or scented the bowhunter. So the deer may work its way along slowly, even though it is bleeding severely. Also such a deer will stop from time to time.

With lung bleeding underway, a time arrives when the amount of blood drawn through the windpipe causes the deer to cough in attempts to clear its air passage. Such coughing can readily be distinguished from the signal or alarm cough, snort or blow emitted when a deer is on the alert. The wounded deer's cough lacks the sharp expelling of air so characteristic of the alarm signal; instead it is muffled, and has a choking sound revealing a struggle for air. Some of the blood withdrawn from the filling lungs eventually will reach the deer's nostrils. This will cause the deer to wheeze or make a bubbling sound as it expels air, sometimes sounding much like a person badly afflicted with a severe head cold who is blowing his nose. Some deer will even sneeze, another symptom of a bad lung wound. So, though the sounds of a deer in flight may not indicate anything especially abnormal, you nevertheless may hear the deer founder and fall.

I find that the broadside shot is rarely presented to the bowhunter. Therefore, practice emphasis should be placed on the quartering angle shots that face both away from and towards the hunter. After years of hunting experience, the bowhunter will find that the profile of the target will vary with each animal.

In general, it is important that bowhunters learn to associate the correct locations of a deer's vital organs. With the bow, a maximum bleeding wound is imperative. The bowhunter cannot rely on any other way of dropping his deer; his methods are denied the shocking powers enjoyed by rifle hunters. So instead, he must place his arrow with precision in a vital part of the deer.

When the arrow has only to penetrate the rib cage in order to get to the lungs, the feat of killing a deer is fairly easy. Rib bones are usually cut by a hunting head, there being very little deflection. In cases where the kind of profile shot offered requires penetration of other organs in order to get an arrow into the lungs, the shot becomes more of a major problem.

Quartering shots do not interpose any great organic barrier. More of a problem, however, is the optical deception experienced by the hunter in the quartering profiles encountered. Although the hunter knows that the animal is not broadside, the common tendency is to try to place the hit too far forward. This usually results in a non-vital hit which passes the lung area and enters the front of the chest thus impacting where it fails to cut any sizable blood vessels. But if the bowhunter will correctly visualize the *angular* anatomy presented and forget about the conventional broadside anatomical arrangement, he can compensate for the quarter angle and make a highly effective hit.

For some reason or another most articles and books on bowhunting or deer hunting with the rifle always have a figure drawing showing the correct positions of heart and lungs in a broadside target. I believe this has done more harm than good to budding bowhunters. As they go forth to the hunting grounds and come upon game targets within shooting range, they try to mentally apply a broadside anatomical picture to the target which, alas, is actually in quite an entirely different line. The result is a badly placed hit. Many wounded deer get away, though not entirely the fault of the hunter. Most of the blame should fall on the many books and articles which persistently give only broadside examples of aiming points.

Rest assured that when you hunt, the odds on encountering a broadside shot are going to be at least five to one against it. Therefore the proper aiming points for all the other possible and more commonly encountered shot angles should be shown and more training emphasis should be given to these variations in aiming point as needed for actual deer hunting. *The bowhunter cannot possibly get his game merely by aiming for the body; he must pick a more precise spot!* This spot must represent the correct point of aim for the angle involved if the arrow is to reach vital organs.

Profiles going directly away present maximum organic arrow barriers. Here the bowhunter's arrow must penetrate the intestinal tract in which the stomach, itself, presents the toughest barrier.

In the case of a deer that has just completed feeding, the stomach is usually so full that it actually is interposed as a miniature bale of straw to obstruct the arrow in such shots. Though it similarly tends to retard a rifle bullet, the stomach's food matter also hastens a bullet's expansion. Penetration of a bullet considered slow to start with would therefore be even less effective and less shock-inducing.

To achieve a lung hit from a shooting position to the rear of a deer, your shaft must penetrate at least twenty inches. Personally, I prefer to see penetration of the arrow as far in as its fletching. On profile targets directly away it is well to place your point of aim just under the base or root of the tail. On away angles the arrow has to contend with a lot of bone structure, so the hunter should try to send the shaft through a point just below the rump bone. If aim is dead correct, the arrow will enter between the hind legs and pass through the top part of the intestines and the stomach, then end as a high hit in the main part of the lungs. Such an arrow deviating high might mean a spine shot or the severing of the aortic artery just under the spine. On the other hand, if the arrow deviates low, it may sever the renal caval or the pyloric artery and be a liver hit. If its penetration is complete it will end up as a heart hit.

If the arrow initially hits high, it can mean a spine shot thus crippling the hind quarters. If the arrow enters tight along the underside of the spine it may cut the aortic artery near where it branches into the femoral leg arteries. Should the archer shoot too high, the arrow may pass over the back of the deer yet still make a highly effective rear neck shot.

On profiles where the deer faces the hunter or is quartering towards the hunter, the arrow must enter the chest. The first organ in its path now will be the lungs where arrow penetration of twelve inches should do the job. I consider that the chances for a spine-injuring hit are good on all game profiles going directly away from or towards the hunter. In the profile facing the hunter, a high arrow may become a possible neck vertebrae hit, or possibly sever a carotid artery. The low arrow then is a possible heart hit, or if to one side, it may still catch the lower lobe of a lung.

The tree hunter, moreover, sees his deer profile from yet an entirely different angle than the foot hunter. If the tree hunter waits for the close-range shot, he has a game profile from almost directly overhead. Seen from this position, the deer's vital organs are much differently arranged than in any of the other profiles. But the overhead shooter must remember to compensate to the right or left in order that his arrow may penetrate lung and heart area. I prefer a point of aim dead center of the back when a deer is directly below me; that is, with an imaginary point of aim centered between the front shoulders and just a shade back. Since I use bone-breaking arrowheads, I shoot for a possible vertebrae and spinal-cord hit. Should the arrow enter either side of the spine, I still can expect a good hit in either the lung or heart area. Most of the time the arrow will go completely through the deer and into the ground beneath him. But, if it breaks the spine it will not of course be able to achieve near that degree of penetration.

In shooting from a tree the bowhunter must remember that he is shooting at a downward angle and compensate for the downward arrow trajectory. This, however, only applies to *other than point blank ranges.* Don't overlook the curve of the deer's sides where they round into the back. Under certain lighting conditions there is a very confusing optical illusion created by the deer's coloration and hair, thus making it difficult to be entirely sure where the deer's back starts and ends.

It is also important to remember to pick only one organ rather than a group of organs as your point of aim. When you pick the heart-lung area and your deer stands giving you plenty of time, pick *either* the lungs *or* the heart but *not both* as your point of aim. Do not merely aim for the general area in which both are found. *You must pick a precise spot and concentrate on that spot only for your shot.* As an aid, associate that precise spot with some specific organ located there. This will help in concentrating while you aim. And picture that deer as a living, three-dimensional, anatomical chart, properly placed to stand in the same relationship to you. Then pinpoint your spot and shoot.

Heart shots, although fatal within short distances, offer only a small target. Since the heart is the pump of the blood system, its injury will quickly produce death. When its function of maintaining circulatory blood pressure through the animal is interrupted, shock is transmitted to many parts of the body. A broadhead arrow penetrating the heart will induce both acute bleeding and extreme shock. Although a very small target, and in most cases mistakenly located by the hunter in aiming, the heart is still the best aiming point because this will allow for a possible high shot scoring in the lungs, and high shots are a common tendency among bowhunters.

Incidentally, when you pick the heart as the vital organ at which to aim, your target is really the size of a grapefruit. This target is also very low in the animal, so low that a misjudgement in aiming can mean a clean miss. And those who consider the heart always to be a perfect target should know that an arrow penetrating only one of the ventricles may allow the deer to run much farther away than it would with a lung hit.

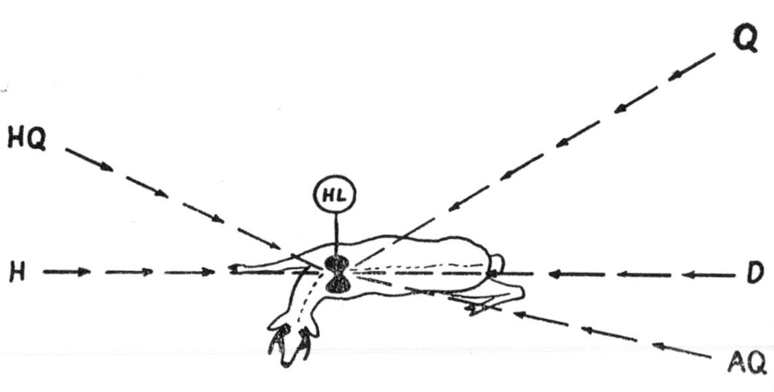

Angles of Target Profile—Where to Place Your Arrow

The top view of the deer, from right to left, illustrates angling shots required from various positions to reach the heart-lung area, marked (HL). The head-on shot (H) requires the same line of sight as the direct away shot (D). The front head-on shot requires only penetration of the chest to reach the lungs, while the direct away (D) requires that the arrow must travel 30 to 36 inches to reach the vital area. The front quartering shot (HQ) must be placed directly in front of the shoulder to reach the vital area. The quartering away shot (Q) requires that the arrow enter the last ribs to angle forward to the lungs. The acute quartering away (AQ) finds the arrow entering just behind the rib cage in order to reach the lung area.

Once I hit a buck in the lower tip of the heart with a rifle bullet, yet it ran ninety-seven yards before falling. When we gave the carcass a final dressing the next day, we found a small piece of hemlock twig in the ventricle of the heart. Shooting a slow bullet (.35 Remington) through a hemlock thicket accounted for this freak condition. Both ventricles had been ruptured at the lower end of the heart, yet this deer kept on going for practically one hundred yards. The walls had undoubtedly collapsed but then they had partially sealed to allow continued pumping action of the heart until other bleeding reached a volume sufficient to down the deer.

Compared to the lungs, which offer a target about the size of a football in place-kick position, the heart really forms a target which greatly reduces the possibility of a good hit. Most heart hits credited to bowhunters occur more through chance, I believe, than through intention. Were the successful heart-shot hunter to confess, he would probably admit having held for the conventional center point of aim, namely the general lung-heart area.

Brain and spine shots, although fatal and dropping your deer within sight, are mostly cases of lucky hits. For these the hunter must be able to get within very close range of the game. From a practical standpoint, this is best possible through use of a tree stand from which the hunter can shoot from above the deer. Then, by picking a spot dead center of the back he can make a crippling spine shot. Also, by placing this spot or point of aim just behind the front shoulders, an arrow deviation to the left or right will still produce a lung or heart hit, sometimes both.

Brain shots offer the toughest shot possible for the bowhunter. They are a similar problem to the rifleman. If the brain pan is missed there is very little surrounding area which offers alternate possibilities. The area *around* the brain is absolutely non-vital in all respects. It is bone and horn structure which offers little if any appreciable possibility for arterial or veinous bleeding; in fact, the head makes a very poor aiming point indeed.

About the only possible effect of a head shot that misses the brain is some momentary stunning. If correctly interpreted, the bowhunter may, with luck, be able to send another arrow into some more vital part of the deer before it recovers.

12

Blood Volume and Shock

TOO MANY deer are left to rot on the hunting grounds each season by hunters who either lack the woodsmanship to follow wounded deer methodically in strange country, or by hunters too inexperienced and uninformed with respect to the game being hunted. The deer thus lost are called "unrecovered deer" by the Game Commission. I speculate that the percentage of such cases may run higher among rifle hunters than among the bowhunters but I do not offer this critically. After all, rifle shooting is long-range work and a hunter is less inclined to walk over to take a look.

But every sincere bowhunter and every sportsman owes it to himself and to the future of our hunting to help hold the "unrecovered deer" statistics to the lowest possible level. To this end there are certain facts concerning a deer's blood volume and its blood trail when wounded that merit the thoughtful consideration of all hunters.

First of all, how much blood does a live healthy deer carry? Precise knowledge concerning this usually obscure fact is most pertinent to the bowhunter, more so than to the "powder burner." The bowhunter's weapon, after all, is fundamentally a blood-letting one. Any shock he hopes to inflict on game must be expected only through causing great and rapid loss of blood. True, this ties in with the need for placing arrows in a vital spot. For this requirement we practice, of course.

But is it possible for a hunter to predict from the blood trail of a wounded deer just how far the animal is yet capable of traveling? Can a hunter expect to do so with accuracy? Many hunters believe so; unfortunately, their predictions are too often far from correct.

The well-defined crimson trail of a wounded deer usually excites these familiar hunter comments: "He can't go far! Look at all the blood he's losing." Or, often heard is, "I just can't understand how that buck kept going; we trailed him for over three hours and you should have seen the pool of blood where he lay down. Then the blood kept getting less and less. Finally, the trail petered out. Never did find him, but I know I made a good hit; why, he must have lost a couple of quarts of blood!"

In studying the trails of wounded deer, you know, or will learn, that unless hotly pursued, a deer will pause to rest after it has fled but a short distance from the geographic locale where shot. If not pressed, the deer may bed down for a while to rest and recuperate, even though it will quickly resume flight if pushed. Hence the bed of a wounded deer will most always contain a pool of blood. Immediately around the impression made by the deer in this bed will also be seen splatters or drippings of blood. These first appear when the deer mills around just before it beds, or later when it moves to resume flight. Mistakenly, most hunters assume the deer is not capable now of more than a few bounds before pitching over dead.

From the hunter's standpoint, blood trail is always important. In bowhunting it is especially important, but it can also be very misleading to the uninformed hunter. Sometimes the trail involves a deer that may actually travel three to four hundred yards before falling. Yet many hunters harbor the conviction that no deer leaving abundant blood trail can live to travel that far. There is, of course, a simple explanation. The quantity of blood left along the trail is simply not sufficient enough, in itself, to cause the deer's collapse.

What is really decisive is the total quantity of blood lost or diverted from the deer's normal circulatory system. This critical loss results from both internal and external bleeding. In most cases, however, the hunter has no way of gauging the extent of internal bleeding. But the latter greatly affects the distance a seriously wounded deer will travel between the place where he was initially wounded and the location where he collapses.

Several years ago I hunted with a group in which one of the bowhunters made a neck hit on a large doe. I surmised the hit to have been made in the fleshy part of the neck because of the relatively short blood trail. The trail petered out rather quickly, and where the deer crossed the road to climb a side ridge, the sign was extremely sparse.

Taking a companion, the hunter who had wounded the deer followed the trail up the side ridge. On locating the spot where the deer had first paused to rest, they found pools of blood as big as a man's hand. But at every point where the deer subsequently paused before resuming flight, the sign fell off to only a few drops now and then.

After trailing the deer over the top of a distant ridge, the hunters completely lost the trail and came back quite puzzled and disgusted. They just simply couldn't understand that it had been possible for this wounded deer to have gone so far; nor could they understand why the blood sign had vanished as they came to the top of the ridge. The hunter who had not recovered his deer insisted that it must now lay dead somewhere on top of the ridge. It was impossible, he proclaimed, for the deer to have gone very far because of all the blood it lost!

Many years ago, I began an impromptu survey concerning such phenomena. Whenever I found myself in conversation with other riflemen and bowhunters alike I asked a question in this vein, "How much blood would you say a deer will lose over a distance of one hundred yards, assuming there was a well-placed lung hit and there is a well-defined blood trail?"

The answers convinced me completely that very few hunters really know how much blood is lost by a wounded deer in making the average blood trail. For that matter, practically none had a good idea concerning the quantity of blood carried by the average live deer. Neither could any of them offer any reasonably accurate guesses concerning the quantity of blood a deer must lose before it reaches a point of involuntary collapse.

The average response to my question dealing with the volume of blood lost over a one-hundred yard trail by a lung-hit was 1½ pints. Extreme guesses ranged from a "full bucket" of blood to as little as a half-pint. And when asked to estimate the volume of blood in a full grown 125-pound buck, the average answer was five gallons! One man, a hunter for over thirty years and one who had taken no less than fifty deer in that time, guessed eight quarts. Close perhaps, but still not necessarily correct.

The correct answer, however, is important because, as we shall see, when a deer loses a certain amount of blood, it must collapse.

Dr. Monica Reynolds, Assistance Professor of Physiology, School of Veterinary Medicine, University of Pennsylvania is known for her work in developing tables dealing with blood, plasma, and red cell volume of bovine animals. One of her works, *Handbook of Biological Data* was published recently by the Federation of American Societies for Experimental Biology, Washington, D. C. Deer are classified as ruminants along with sheep, cows, and goats; and since a deer's anatomy is reasonably similar to others of the group in enough respects, Dr. Reynolds feels safe in assuming a deer's blood volume can be arrived at through methods similar to those used in compiling data for most of the other animals of the group. Her opinion, therefore, is that a deer's blood volume will run approximately thirty cubic centimeters, or one ounce for each pound of the deer's total weight.

Dr. Stanley C. Whitlock, Assistant Chief of the Game Division, State of Michigan has the following to say concerning the blood volume of whitetail deer: "Generally speaking, about eight percent of the animal's weight is made up of blood. Therefore, a 100-pound deer would be expected to carry approximately eight pounds, or roughly eight pints of blood."

He also adds that a deer of this weight would be seriously weakened by the loss of one pint of blood. Loss of two pints of blood would stop the same deer, in most instances producing shock and quite probably death. He also notes that in cases where the blood is lost slowly, the animal will tend to compensate for the loss far easier than if the blood is lost suddenly as through hemorrhage from the cutting of a large artery.

The considered opinion of Dr. John E. Martin, Assistant to the Dean, School of Veterinary Medicine, University of Pennsylvania, relative to a deer's loss of blood and to shock is to this effect: "Loss of slightly more than one-third of the total volume of blood induces shock to the degree that the animal will fall."

In a report concerning archery hunting recently submitted to Mr. William E. Warne, Director of the California Department of Fish and Game, appeared the following interesting statement attributed to Mr. Gerald E. Eddy, Director of the Game Department of Michigan: "An arrow kills differently than a bullet. Profuse bleeding usually occurs while shock, with the exception of being hit in the spine or the brain, is negligible. If a large blood vessel is not severed and the body cavity not punctured, the chances for complete recovery are good. The arrow usually breaks off or falls out and the wound may heal over, leaving the head of the arrow imbedded and walled off by a natural growth of tissue, just as may occur with a bullet."

When I discussed the shock effect of arrows with Dr. Mark Allam, Dean of the School of Veterinary Medicine, University of Pennsylvania, he remarked that ". . . Shock results from a derangement in the circulatory and nervous systems. No one weapon will create a more severe state of shock than the other, providing both weapons penetrate the body at the same point, in the same manner."

Most hunters are generally agreed that the high-powered rifle bullet inflicts far more shock on game than will the hunting arrow. The genesis of this view probably is linked with examinations of game which make it clear that the wound channel of a bullet is far larger than that left by the average arrow. The bullet, therefore, is presumed to destroy more tissue than does the penetrating broadhead. We can do better than speculate, however. Sandbox tests also help us see the differences.

If a high-powered rifle is loaded with the usual hunting ammunition, then fired into a box of sand eight-inches deep, its bullet will not pass entirely through the sand but expand, instead. The bullet's energy will spend itself through expansion and friction as it moves forward against the sand. It then is brought to a stop only a short distance from the point of its entrance. But a hunting arrow from a fifty-pound bow will pass through the same sandbox easily; the arrow does not expand, hence its energy is fully applied to penetration.

If we substitute flesh for sand, the bullet will tear and destroy much tissue as it expands and penetrates. This is what it was designed to do. In contrast, the arrow passes through the same kind of flesh with little damage to surrounding tissue. Pain also induces shock; from this standpoint, too, the bullet rather than the arrow is more shock-inducing because it shatters more bone and thus also damages more tissue.

In summary, a deer's traumatic injuries from a rifle bullet extend over a greater area than from the arrow. The bullet's larger wound channel also results in more profuse internal hemorrhage. In many cases the deer shot by a rifle will not take more than a step or two before keeling over. Some even collapse in their tracks. Pooling of blood in the deer's abdomen usually commences simultaneous with the bullet wound; it thus may occur, in fact, instantaneously.

The bowhunter inflicts the wound of lesser size. The arrow wound is limited by the width of the broadhead and the diameter of the shaft. It therefore produces lesser traumatic injury, shock, and internal hemorrhage. The deer shot by an arrow must be expected to travel a greater distance after being shot than if shot instead with a rifle bullet.

Over the years I have frequently been curious about the quantitative significance of various blood trails left by wounded game. Often, whiling away the minutes in some unremunerative tree stand, the useful mathematics, if any, which might be invoked to help a hunter outguess a wounded deer's travels engaged my speculative thought. Sometimes this led on with yet indolent speculation that one might perhaps sometime devise a useful clue, formula, or experiment by which to enhance the chances of recovering wounded deer. Other hunters, no doubt, under the same circumstances have day-dreamed the same way.

Such patterns of thought bob along pretty much in the same way: Killing deer by bow and arrow involves blood-letting and blood loss. A healthy deer has a fixed quantity of blood, the quantity obviously varies from one deer to the next. When a deer loses a certain part of this quantity he must collapse. The wounded deer leaves a blood trail; the quantity of blood varies among such trails. The wounded deer also bleeds internally. This amount, too, is a variable. Assuming A is the quantity representing a healthy deer's normal blood volume, C can represent its critical fraction which, if lost, causes the deer to collapse. The quantity of external bleeding shows along the trail; let EB stand for this. Internal bleeding must be considered; call it IB. Rates of bleeding are involved, too; now a time element complicates the business. Old questions crop up. Several factors are concerned now. Regarding

A=Who knows how much; surely it varies from deer to deer?
C=Again, who knows? Yet,
A–C=A deer quite probably in the hunter's bag. And
C=EB+IB; maybe even IB or EB alone, in rare though possible cases.
EB=Can it ever be measured? Approximated?
IB=Only assumptions seem possible.

To further such speculations along more practical lines more facts and notes were needed than I had been in the habit of keeping, but eventually, several winters ago, I decided to experiment with EB. So, as objectively as possible, review with me if you will some experimental blood trails deliberately made with fact finding in mind. They were made to resemble those left by wounded deer and laid on a good ground layer of December snow. This was in typical deer country; some trails ran a measured 100 yards, others 150 yards.

The deer blood simulated in the trails was made with a domestic form of beef blood to which I added enough citrate of soda to avoid coagulation. The consistency of the resultant marking fluid was probably a bit heavier than would be the case with actual whitetail blood, but on the whole, I think, there resulted a fairly good approximation. All applications of the fluid were liberal.

TRAIL A
(100 Yards)

WOUND SIMULATED: Lung hit, arrow passing completely through deer.

PATTERN: Spurts of fluid were applied three to four feet on each side of trail; extra-heavy spurts were made to represent the beginning of the trail.

FLUID APPLIED: 2.25 ounces, slightly over 1/8 pint.

Hypothetical Case–128-Pound Deer

To estimate this deer's proximity to collapse from external blood loss:

a. Deer's estimated blood volume: 128 ounces, or 4 quarts.
b. Estimated loss required for collapse: 43 ounces, or about 2¾ pints.
c. Estimated external loss (from simulated trail): 2.25 ounces, slightly over 1/8 of a pint.
d. Volume yet to be lost before deer's collapse is imminent (b. – c.): 40.75 ounces, or about 2½ pints.

Remarks: We may estimate this deer will collapse within the 100-yard trail distance only if internal bleeding occurs to the extent of losing 40.75 ounces of blood, as indicated in d. above.

The rate of external bleeding is .0225 ounces per yard (average). The rate of internal bleeding necessary to the deer's collapse within this trail distance is .4075 ounces per yard. Note that the ratio between the calculated internal and external bleeding rates would have to be rather high, 18 to 1. Should we expect to find this deer close by?

TRAIL B
(100 yards)

WOUND SIMULATED: Hard-hit deer. Not necessarily a lung hit, but wounded to the extent of leaving a very well-defined trail indicative of arterial or other heavy bleeding, the arrow having passed completely through the deer.

PATTERN: Generous spatters of fluid were used, especially in the area representing trail's beginning.

FLUID APPLIED: 11 ounces, just under ¾ pint.

Hypothetical Case A—100-Pound Deer

To estimate this deer's proximity to collapse from external blood loss:

a. Deer's estimated blood volume: 100 ounces, or about 6⅛ pints.
b. Estimated loss required for collapse: 35 ounces, or about 2⅛ pints.
c. Estimated external loss (from simulated trail): 11 ounces, slightly less than ¾ pint.
d. Volume yet to be lost before deer's collapse is imminent (b. – c.): 24 ounces, or about 1½ pints.

Remarks: Through only external bleeding, this deer would have lost slightly less than 1/3 the quantity of blood required to induce shock and collapse within the trail distance.

Hypothetical Case B—150-Pound Deer

This deer would have to lose 52 ounces, or about 3¼ pints of blood before collapse. Internal blood loss would have to extend to 41 ounces, or about 2½ pints to stop the deer within the trail distance. In other words, the internal loss rate would have to be almost four times that of the external rate in order to down the deer. (Average internal blood loss needed would be .41 ounces per yard; the external rate, .11 ounces per yard.)

TRAIL C
(150 yards)

WOUND SIMULATED: "Non-vital" hit such as hind-quarter hit, neck wound, high back hit, etc. Some bleeding from vein severance; dripping along the trail evident.

PATTERN: Little if any hemorrhaging occurs in lesser hits; the trail was laid out through drippings to simulate no profuse bleeding areas. Gut-shot deer sometimes leave a trail of this kind.

FLUID APPLIED: One ounce, or 1/16 pint.

Hypothetical Case—128-Pound Deer

This deer would have to lose 42 ounces of blood, about 2 3/5 pints, to fall by the trail's end. The rate of external bleeding is computed as .007 ounces per yard (average). Assuming the rate of internal bleeding to be at a two to one ratio, it would still average only a loss rate of .014 ounces per yard.

Remarks: This trail represents no profuse bleeding wound nor hemorrhaging, so if we conservatively assume this deer bled internally at a two to one ratio, it would still have lost only three ounces, or about 1/5 pint of blood by the time it reached the end of the 150-yard trail. This slight loss would be well below the amount estimated to cause the animal's collapse. In fact this deer could travel very close to 2,000 yards, or better than one and one-seventh miles, before collapsing from such a wound. True, if not pushed or disturbed, this deer may bed within a relatively short distance from the locale where shot. This would tend to shorten its distance of travel considerably. If the wound continues to bleed after the deer beds down, the deer will likely become weak and stiff, thus it would be hampered in moving any great distance. In such a case, if the hunter allows some waiting time, then tracks the deer, he may, true enough, get a good chance for a second and more telling shot.

TRAIL D

SITUATION SIMULATED: The bed of a wounded deer, assuming liberal bleeding.

PATTERN: Usually there is a pool of blood where the deer has lain, also spatters and drippings. A pool 12-inches in diameter was reproduced. Since the fluid soaked down through the snow, more of an application was needed than one might think necessary in order to secure the pooling effect.

FLUID APPLIED: Six ounces, or about 3/8 of a pint.

Hypothetical Case A

If the volume of fluid used was *combined* with that of the Trail A case, the total consumed would still be less than nine ounces, slightly over ½ pint. This suggests that a deer wounded as in Trail A could still travel a considerable distance even though it were to bed down temporarily.

For example, if a 128-pound deer was wounded as in Trail A, then ran for fifty yards and bedded down, it would have lost 1.125 ounces, or about 1/16 pint of blood via its external trail. A total loss of 7.125 ounces or about ½ pint of blood is assumed if we add the six ounces lost in the bed. Ignoring any accompanying internal loss of blood, one can readily see that this deer might run another fifty to seventy-five yards if jumped again by the hunter in too short a time. But the blood loss would still be far less than the forty-three ounces necessary to cause its early collapse.

Hypothetical Case B–128-Pound Deer

Assume this deer ran the full distance of 150-yards and then bedded down after receiving a "non-vital" wound such as in Trail C. A loss of one ounce of blood is estimated via the external blood trail. Adding the six ounces of blood lost in a bedded situation, the total external blood lost would be seven ounces. If internal blood loss occurred at a two to one ratio, a conservative assumption, we may assume the internal loss to be fourteen ounces (or about 7/8 of a pint). The aggregate blood loss, internal as well as external, would still amount to only twenty-one ounces, or about 1 1/3 pints. Note that this is still less than half the amount estimated as required to cause the deer's collapse (43 ounces, or about 2¾ pints).

If left undisturbed for a time with the wound continuing to bleed at about the same rate, the chances are this deer could be recovered by the hunter. But if bleeding continues at a slow rate the animal will not weaken rapidly. Too, if the wound is merely a surface one, there would be some likelihood of the blood coagulating through air contact and perhaps eventual healing.

Bleeding sometimes ceases, of course, because of the compression of the deer's body against the ground when bedded. No doubt some coagulation or wound plugging also results through contact of the deer's body with leaves or moss on the ground.

The gist of it all is merely to illustrate why the bowhunter shouldn't be too surprised if his wounded deer is finally recovered quite a distance from the place of shooting. The wise bowhunter therefore should be prepared to carry out a search for his wounded deer over an extensive area. Thought provoking as these cases might be, exact parallels in actual hunting should not always be expected; deer hunting is too variable for that.

But let us suppose a hunter puts his arrow through the chest of a buck, severing the anterior aortic artery, passing through the top lobe of a lung, and lodging in the liver. Such a hit is ideal indeed, for the internal blood loss may well be triple that of some of the cases about which we have speculated. Then, the chances are that the buck will not make more than a few leaps and fall within sight of the hunter.

A deer's temperament as well as his general condition also has a lot to do with the rather surprising stamina he sometimes displays. For example, a wounded or highly excited deer may be so supercharged with its own adrenalin as to enable it to run much farther than it might if it received the same hit while relaxed and feeding. Then, too, bear in mind that the arrow that passes completely through the deer increases the rate of hemorrhage and reduces the yardage of wound trails. The opposite also is true; less arrow penetration means less blood vessels severed.

Nor will any two deer react exactly the same way when wounded. Neither will they very often present identical kinds of targets. All this, of course, is part and parcel of what makes bowhunting so challenging. It exacts every bit of knowhow from the hunter.

We can sum it up though, by saying the bowhunter who thoughtfully applies his field experience and studies the possibilities suggested by these experimental trails should have less than average difficulty with the recovery of wounded deer. By applying his knowledge and carefully studying the trail sign he will have a decided edge over the many hunters who believe wounded deer will always be found very close at hand.

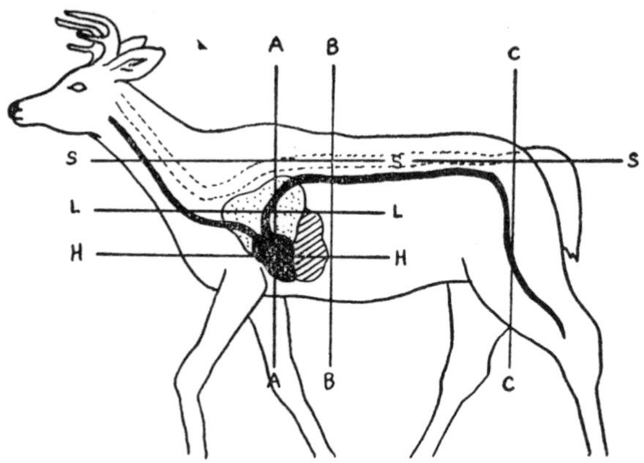

Vital Areas for Point of Aim

The heart and main anterior and posterior arteries, including the femoral artery, are shown in black; the lungs, which extend down over the heart on each side, are shown in dotted area; while the liver, low and behind the heart, is shown in striped area, with the spine shown as the broken line from head to tail.

Vertical line (A) designates the maximum forward deflective line of sighting which puts the arrow in the center of the heart-lung cluster as well as the top exit of the aortic arteries. Hits to the left or forward will strike the shoulder-bone which will prevent penetration. Vertical line (B) designates the maximum deflective line of sighting to the right or rear of line (A), which is about nine inches in distance. A hit between (A) and (B) if low or at cross-hair line (H) will result in either a heart or liver hit. If hit between (A) and (B) center at cross-hair line (L) the hit will be in the rear of the lung lobe. If hit anywhere along cross-hair line (S) between deflective line (A) to (C) the arrow will strike the spine. A hit where (H) and (A) intersect means a dead center heart shot. If the arrow enters where (L) and (A) intersect, the center of the lungs will be hit, and also a possible severance of the posterior aortic artery as well. An arrow that hits in the area of deflective line (C) down through the center of the hind ham will sever the femoral artery. With the exception of the spine hits all the other vital points will produce sufficient hemorrhage to drop the deer within reasonable yardage.

13

Unorthodox Shots

WITH A FEW exceptions perhaps, most archers have had the disappointing experience of missing shots at game while hunting. What "rubs the salt in the wound" is the fact that in most cases these misses occur at comparatively close-range distances at which the archer is usually quite consistent and in most cases highly accurate.

The expert AA or A-class archer could in most cases place his shots in the five-ring at the range he missed his game. Why the clean miss at distances as near as fifteen to twenty yards? Many contributing factors help create this condition.

(1) Cover and terrain offering few and small openings.

(2) Movement and behavior of game.

(3) Unexpected appearance of game in places other than in front of the archer.

(4) Amount of light available at the time of the shot and the type of weather controlling this light.

(5) Emotional condition of the archer.

(6) Knowledge of the game being hunted.

(7) Amount of hunting experience.

(8) Aiming for the whole deer instead of picking a spot to hit.

(9) The most important of all, the lack of ability of the archer to take advantage of a possible shot from other than an orthodox position.

Top shooting classes are composed of archers who have developed a consistent form of release and "locking in" of the bow arm. Stance is varied among the individual shooters but always consistent in minute detail. Shooting for score is usually done with light tackle and sensitive aluminum arrows. As a rule the archer holds long, locking the bow arm for steady release. This is all fine for field-course shooting, but such practices do not allow for the conditions that prevail in hunting.

So let's consider some differences in shooting which are to be expected between the target shooter and the hunting archer.

Cover and Terrain: In shooting the conventional N.A.A. field target course the instinctive archer faces targets from ten to eighty yards in distance. Some of these may be downhill and some uphill, but in most cases the fairway or path from the shooting stake to the target butt is comparatively free of any obstacles.

When hunting in timber or brushy terrain, the bowhunter may be required to find his own openings and send his shaft through some which are as small as twelve inches. Faced with this handicap, the archer who is accustomed to field course shooting *only* is at a definite disadvantage.

In early October 1960, after having returned from a western elk hunting trip, I was still able to get in two weeks of Pennsylvania bowhunting. The second day turned out to be a rainy and foggy morning, a fact I noted as I rose for breakfast. It was very similar, in fact, to that same day in the year immediately preceding. In thought I relived the incident.

I had played a hunch, that morning of '59, as I worked my way along the dirt road to slowly approach the first clearing. Fog and poor light had made me wait until ten minutes after legal shooting time. Visibility was still extremely limited but getting to the edge of the clearing, I checked, peering intently through the brush and thicket bordering the opening. After advancing twice and checking each time, I spotted the ghost-like outline of a deer in the fog. Watching, I estimated the distance to be about fifty yards but the extremely poor light, fog, and rain made the exact range questionable. As I carefully looked for an opening to shoot through I observed that the deer was moving slowly in a normal feeding manner. Carefully checking what little air movement existed, I was glad to note that luckily I was standing downwind of the deer. Finding what I hoped was an opening of sufficient size to shoot through, I raised my bow but noted that the overhead brush would not permit a conventional bow position. So I canted the bow extremely to allow for limb room, then from a forward stooping position, drew and anchored my shaft. Holding for an imaginary spot dead center of the front quarter, I raised slightly to compensate for possible underestimation of distance and loosed the arrow.

At the moment of the release the deer took a step forward, then came the sound of the arrow hitting solid muscle coupled with the alarmed snort of the deer to verify a hit. In a flash, the deer bounded out of sight as I ran into the opening and glimpsed three white flags vanishing into the fog and misty rain.

I noticed that one of the three tails was erratic in flight, weaving back and forth until out of sight and I assumed this to be the hit deer. I also suspected a hit towards the rear of the whitetail with little bleeding likely to leave external sign. Familiar with the country, I ran down to the lower end of the clearing, about eighty yards away. I realized as I ran that with the steady rain and wet ground any blood trail would be washed away within minutes.

Getting to the righthand corner of the lower end of the clearing, I checked the exit run that led across the dirt road into heavy thicket. Kneeling in the rain, I examined the ground for fresh sharp prints or for any sign of blood. To see, it was necessary to bend quite close to the ground because of the still extremely poor light that prevailed. But there was not a fresh print or any blood sign to be found. Rising, I turned and headed towards the opposite corner of this end of the clearing where I knew another exit run was located. Halfway across, I noticed what appeared to be a clump of brush. After having nocked another arrow, I carefully approached this strange outline in the mist. When I got within forty yards I was able to distinguish the outline of a deer lying on the ground; it was my deer, down but not dead. Approaching with bow ready, I found the deer not able to rise. It was then dispatched by an arrow to the neck near the base of the head.

My first arrow had hit the center of a hind ham at the same elevation as I had held for on the chest area. The femoral arteries were severed as the arrow passed through both hams. The shaft had been thrown at the point where the buck turned at the lower end of the clearing; the arrow had worked back out by the action of the deer's powerful leg muscles as he ran. This deer traveled a total distance of one hundred yards after being hit.

Case and point: This shot necessitated a position completely unorthodox to basic archery shooting and could not otherwise have been made in view of the cover and terrain.

Now, a year later, and on another morning with rain and fog making conditions identical to the previous season, I headed for the same mountain road and clearing in the hope that history would repeat. Slowly working along the dirt road I carefully checked the clearing from upper to lower end. But not a deer was to be seen until I reached the lower end where the run led across the road and into the thicket. Then, glancing into the thicket to my right, I spotted a movement. I dropped to my haunches and remained motionless, eyes searching the thicket maize. Yes, there he was! No more than forty yards away, entirely unaware of me, was a browsing six-pointer.

Afraid to move, since at times he looked directly at me, I kept as low as possible to avoid presenting a silhouette. Meanwhile I kept looking for a possible opening through which to send an arrow. Finally, after checking every possible angle, I decided to try what seemed to be an open twelve-inch corridor through the saplings and brush. I had to shoot from a kneeling position; there was no other way. Even then, I had to invert the bow so I could get close to ground level, for at most this opening ran only about thirty inches above the ground. Thus, with bow limbs parallel to the ground, my head canted hard right and sighting along the under side of the bow, I made the release. Sure enough, the arrow sped through the opening and true towards the front quarter of the buck. But the shaft hit a small sapling directly in front of the buck and deflecting, buried itself in the ground between the buck's front feet.

Case and point: This shot had required an extremely unorthodox position in order to try to get the shaft through the available opening. The assumed position and the shot were perfect; the miss was due to an obstacle outside my range of visibility, so I can only term this as a "successful miss."

Tree shooting requires varied unorthodox shooting positions. I have both killed and missed deer from various awkward positions while tree hunting. Almost always tree hunting requires an unorthodox position and offers only limited openings through which the hunter may try his shot.

While hunting in Pennsylvania with Howard Hill during the '59 season, we did some night coon hunting. This is a real way to test your ability to send an arrow through a small opening. Shooting at a coon that is clinging to the very tips of tree branches some thirty to forty feet high with only its eyes shining in the rays of the spotlight and with foliage hiding the body requires that you judge the position of the body, place your imaginary point of aim within that assumed body, and employ full instinctive judgment in aiming, since there is no possible sighting picture to help. To top all other handicaps you must employ some very unorthodox shooting positions. There are overhead branches to contend with, ground underfoot, and it is difficult to find a good opening as a clear path for your arrow to reach the target. I got the first coon with one arrow, but misjudged and missed several after that.

Movement and behavior of game: The target archer, when stepping up to the shooting stake, faces a stationary target with but one factor to contend with: wind drift. Wild game, on the other hand, very seldom remains motionless, especially when being stalked. Usually aware of the hunter's presence, game is nervous and spooky, ready for flight to safety. The result is a target that either moves erratically, runs swiftly, or keeps sneaking along through cover. So the target presents problem combinations of wind-drift handicap, the targets are moving erratically, and there are few openings through which the bowhunter can place his shot quickly and accurately. When there are openings, they are apt to be very small ones.

Because of the many unpredictable moves that game make, the bowhunter must condition himself to shoot quickly when necessary. A buck may present a perfect target for an instant, then change position or step into cover, thus making a seemingly good shot practically impossible. The experienced bowhunter wastes as little time as possible, drawing and releasing his arrow knowing well the true fickleness of the game target.

An experience that many beginning bowhunters have to face up to and endure, is "sweating" a deer within shooting range and then finding themselves unable to send an arrow to the target because of position. The important thing to remember in such a case is that it may still be possible to make a shot, but that it must be one from an unorthodox position. Instead of being forced to let the deer get away in such a situation because of unfamiliarity with such shots, the hunter who has practiced such positions until fairly accurate will have a decided edge to handle the seemingly impossible shot.

While hunting deer one season I kept working a certain cultivated field which rested on top of a ridge completely surrounded by timber. This field was a game favorite for early evening feeding; it was visited by a group of deer practically every day. There was an abundant mixture of field clover and timothy. About dusk the deer would appear. My only problem was coping with the constantly changing wind currents on the ridgetop; it seemed that at any run I would post myself, the deer would get my scent and enter the field from another point. Also, once in the field, it was impossible to stalk the deer within shooting range without being detected.

This group of deer was being herded by an old doe which

had a crippled hind leg, and I really wanted to get her very badly. Up to this time I had not seen her in full flight but judging by her way of walking and loping, I felt obligated to try to put her out of, what I considered, a handicapped life. After several very unsuccessful evening trys I decided to give an entirely unorthodox, if not downright foolish method, a try.

I had observed that these deer were very consistent, they would always work towards a certain point in the field, one which happened to be at the center of a slight swell, so I figured on being there to greet them. Removing my quiver but taking along one extra arrow, I worked my way into the center of this swell which was so popular with the deer. Picking a spot on its edge, I lay down flat on my face in a patch of timothy, now dressed in green trousers, a camouflage jacket, and with mud smeared on my face, I settled down to wait.

This particular piece of land was not being hunted by other bowhunters. Since it was posted, it did not present safety problems. As a matter of fact, were any hunter to enter the land to hunt even without the permission of its owner, the chances were that he would hunt along the edge of the clearing.

Yet very few bowhunters would entertain the thought of trying what I had in mind that afternoon. Or, should I say that at least very few of them in their right mind would? But past-hunting experiences have proved to me that even the foolish way sometimes bears fruit.

I was concealed by the timothy which stood about ten to twelve inches high. By keeping my head down most of the time and only raising it to check for deer, I was not exposed. In fact, I was able to blend into the cover quite effectively. Too, I relied upon the fact that deer would not expect any danger in this part of the field, since all previous disturbances by the hunter had been made along the edges of the field adjoining the timber. The whitetails would remember to check that area consistently for danger.

As six o'clock approached I had a half-hour of hunting time left. There was adequate daylight, even after legal shooting time was over, since daylight saving time was then still in effect. This would allow ample time to trail a wounded deer without worry of darkness intervening.

From time to time I slowly raised my head and checked around but no deer were in sight. Turning my head from left to right I kept telling myself they were not coming out in time tonight. But then suddenly I spotted the head and alert ears of a doe looking right at me. Keeping my head mostly down in the top of the timothy, I raised often enough to study her as best I could in brief glimpses as she stood about forty yards away looking directly towards me. As a test to determine if she had spotted my movements, I slowly eased my head back into the timothy and lay flat on my face for several minutes. Then rising again slowly so as not to betray any movement, I looked in her direction. There she stood, a statue of alert suspicion as she curiously studied this strange object that intermittently showed over the grass tips.

My bow was ready, along my right side with arrow nocked. But I kept watching her, realizing that it would be impossible to try for a shot while she was in this position. As I waited, I noticed that the other deer were feeding unconcernedly. This verified my hunch that the doe watching me was more curious than frightened. So I decided to play upon her curiosity and to try to entice her closer to me, relying on a chance to make a shot when she moved.

Finally the familiar trait of her species prompted her to take a step in my direction. Head forward and with ears pointed in my direction she stomped her forefoot and signalled an alert to the others. While she stopped again trying to figure me out, I remained flat on my face for several seconds, trying to tease her into coming closer. But then she changed her tactics and decided to employ her more sensitive tools. Circling slowly in a stiff-legged manner, she kept working around to the back of me, sniffing and waiting for a telltale scent to verify her suspicions. With the wind directly to my rear she had to complete a one hundred and eighty degree arc before arriving at a downwind position. Then she was about thirty yards in back of me, still not fully alarmed but busy looking and snorting.

I decided it was now or never, so I slowly tried to pivot about in a prone position and bringing my bow around with me. My hopes were for a sitting shot while she presumably bounced away, probably at a range of no more than sixty yards. The doe tolerated my slow pivoting motions but spooked when I arrived at a sitting position. My shot was at around fifty yards and of course it had to be a quick one. But the arrow was low and stuck in the ground directly in front of her; she actually stumbled over it while running away. Only then did I discover she had no trouble with her "bad hind leg" when she really wanted to "pour on the coal."

As she and the rest of the deer vanished into the timber I

chuckled, rose, and stretched my stiff muscles. My miss had been close, my plan had worked, and I was just a bit glad for having missed after seeing her move so well at a full run. When I headed for the car with the bow unstrung, I was completely satisfied with the hunt.

Case and point: As wild as the idea seems, here had been a chance to try a very unorthodox shot from a sitting position. Having practiced such shots many times I recognized their existence but slim possibility of connecting. However, in such a situation the bowhunter who has not practiced other than conventional standing shots would not usually be able to get an arrow anywhere within even close proximity of the deer.

Unexpected appearance of game: As any experienced hunter can testify, game has the habit of appearing in the most unlikely places at times which catch the hunter relaxing and off-balance. When this happens the bowhunter does not have time to assume a proper shooting stance and he must make a quick shot from a very abnormal position if he is to shoot at all.

Deer have an uncanny habit of stepping into a hunter's view at the most unpredictable places and times. The bowhunter may be facing one way and the deer will appear from behind or from the left or the right of the hunter. Often a deer will step into view too close to permit the hunter to turn and assume a proper stance facing the game, so he must adapt himself to the shooting position by twisting his torso and arms. Sometimes this movement is possible at a proper time, however, the noise of the hunter's feet moving in dry leaves may spook the deer.

In the case of a deer that approaches the hunter from behind, drawing and turning must be performed as nearly in one coordinated movement as possible. This will afford a good snapshot at a target which then is usually not moving too fast. At times it will catch a deer flat-footed and thus you may get a chance at a very surprised but still stationary whitetail.

Of course there is always the proverbial deer that has been standing within several yards of you for minutes watching for some telltale movement. Partially concealed in the foliage perhaps you feel its intent stare as you turn your head in its direction. Frequently, some kind of a duel then takes place between the deer and the hunter. Each tries to outstare the other! The bowhunter who has had such experience before will be very busy at the same time he is staring in studying all details of the area so that he can plan his possible moves when and if the break comes his way.

Some other noise may then distract the deer for a second. If this happens, the bowhunter must move quickly and quietly. With the least possible movement he must raise his bow and shoot. If he has no chance to do this before the deer bolts, he is mentally prepared for other possible shots as the deer gets underway. The terrain and cover will influence the manner and direction of the deer's flight. Heavy cover with a run leading out may cause the deer to make a quick turn and flee back into the same protective cover from which he just emerged. Open timber allows flight in practically any direction. Deer escape tactics on side ridges follow a pattern of up and over if the deer is moving along the side, or along the side if the deer is coming up. In most cases the deer going down will turn back in the direction from which it came.

Light conditions: Visibility plays a more important part in good shooting than most archers will admit. There are days in a club shoot or in a mere round of course shooting when the shooter's score will drop below average. Most archers will shrug their shoulders, blaming it on an "off day." But often the real culprit is bad light. Overcast or bright sunny days strongly affect the bowhunter's depth perception and estimation of distance. In the big timber back or side lighting on the colors camouflaging game produces optical illusions for the bowhunter which can result in a miss, yet were he to return later that same day and get the same shot but with the sun in a different position, he might score a hit. Early morning and late evening shots present many handicaps because available light is limited. Rainy weather or heavily overcast days also change the sighting picture.

With snow as a background, a bright sunny day causes glaring reflections similar in effect for the bowhunter as the heat wave distortions occurring on hot summer days.

The natural camouflage that game animals are endowed with through color and shape is accented under certain light conditions. Sunlight, for example, will often reflect from a deer in a way which distorts its body outline. Overcast and rainy days produce optical illusions in which deer look larger, therefore seemingly closer. A wet deer looks darker, thus appearing farther away than it really is. The appearance of a bedded deer often deceives the hunter. Unless the deer is spotted broadside, the hunter may have trouble determining whether the deer is facing him or lying the opposite way.

Overheated deer which have run quite a distance in cold weather emit a slight body vapor, similar to that which humans sometimes emit in the same temperatures when perspiring and overheated. If it is cold enough, this body vapor actually assumes the semblance of a mild cloud form. At distances of forty to fifty yards this can mean quite a parallax problem to the shooters, especially if the deer is standing in a patch of bright sunlight.

During the last few minutes of the hunting day and after sunset the dusk condition gives rise to many deceiving light problems. But I adhere to a policy of not shooting at a deer during the last half-hour of daylight even though hunting regulations permit, and I recommend you do likewise. Then tracking time is limited and the recovery of a whitetail becomes a very questionable matter. Remember there is almost always a next day in which to resume hunting and in which there will be many more hours of daylight for tracking and recovering deer.

Pre-sunrise hunting is another tricky time as far as lighting conditions are concerned and many western states permit such early hunting. But deer which are spotted while the first rays of sunlight filter through the overhead foliage often present optical illusion such as manifested by halo outlines. Then a hunter's concentration on a particular spot on the deer is hard to accomplish because of the blurred and indefinite body outline.

Another very unique phenomenon encountered in forest hunting is the magnification of objects by rain droplets brought about when sunlight hits these crystal globules. Hunting after a rainfall is usually a propitious time for the still hunter, since then there is a quiet carpet of wet leaves to muffle the sounds of footsteps. But there can be optical deceptions in sighting game through openings in wet timber. As the sunlight picks up the myriad of droplets clinging to the leaves, the reflections are magnified tremendously. This too, makes for a deceiving perspective, especially in estimating range. Too often the bowhunter will underestimate the distance. Rifle hunters encounter much the same misleading lighting conditions. But with their rifles they also possess a greater permissable range and margin of error than the bowhunter.

Emotional condition of the archer: Other than the strain of competition in shooting the field course, the archer is usually relaxed, but when hunting, the direct opposite applies. Tense and extremely alert in hunting, he must concentrate on making minimum movement and noise and to remain concealed from the wary eyes of game. The sudden appearance of game may startle him, then his glands pump an extra charge of adrenalin into his blood stream and this often creates a supercharged emotional condition. Individual reactions then become quite variable. "Buck fever" is the common term for the ailment. Many stories tell of the abnormal actions of hunters under this emotional stress. The bowhunter in this supercharged condition is likely to flinch, overdraw, or momentarily freeze as a shot presents itself.

Being in a good position to observe such a humorous incident several years ago, I watched this kind of reaction in a hunting companion. We were in the process of working our way along a narrow woodland trail across a mountaintop, which having been timbered quite heavily some years back, now attracted quite a few deer in its slashings. Several hundred yards before getting to a clearing where we intended to still-hunt for apple-feeding deer, lay a huge pile of sawdust left by the earlier timbering crews. A small clearing surrounded the sawdust. Instead of stepping into the clearing, however, I stepped to the side of the trail and stopped, concealed behind a huge beech. As my companion approached, I allowed him to pass me unnoticed and step into the clearing. Slowly he passed through the opening, his bow ready with arrow nocked, heading for the trail on the opposite side. Unknown to me, a doe stood on the farther side of the clearing in the midst of a clump of withers-high, dead, brown brush. As my companion passed slowly looking around, he failed to spot her as she waited motionless for him to pass before she broke away. When my fellow bowhunter had reached a point several steps past her, she exploded out of the cover. The surprised reaction of the hunter was indeed something that would have made a prize photograph! As he spun in his tracks and faced the deer, he unconsciously allowed the arrow to jump out of its nocking position on the string, but then pulling the bow back to anchor position he realized that he had not brought back an arrow along with the string. Instead, he was holding the arrow in his bowhand similar to the way he normally would when walking along in the usual position ready for drawing. By then, of course, the deer was gone and I gave myself away with hearty laughter. But the incident was amusing to my companion, too. And this was, of course, a perfect example of how the emotional reactions of a hunter can be when suddenly confronted with game.

Yet on suddenly seeing a deer another bowhunter of my acquaintance took his arrow out of nock and off the bow, put it into his shoulder quiver and drew a fresh shaft. Luckily this doe was very cooperative. After nocking this arrow, he drew and shot, then collected the deer after seventy yards of tracking!

This man had never hunted with the bow before but had many years of hunting with a rifle under his belt. His comment on this occasion was, "I shot many a buck with the rifle and never had a touch of buck fever. I sure did not think that a doe could do this to me." So one just never knows when the "fever" may occur; but, by the same token, no one should dread its possibility, for this is all part of true hunting enjoyment.

So far, I have never had a case of buck fever hit me at the time of shooting game. But I did have a sort of "post-operative" case of buck fever many years ago, about the time I killed my first nice buck with a rifle. Perfectly calm all the time in bagging this buck, I was seized with a violent case of shivering when I got ready to field-dress my trophy. It became so acute that when a passing hunter stopped to admire the buck, I was unable even to speak distinctly. Now, many years and many bucks later, I still look back on this experience as my only real brush with that deer-hunter's malady known as "buck fever." It is proof positive that hunting is thrilling.

Knowledge of game hunted: Experience is a great asset when the unexpected happens afield. Knowing how to find deer, their feeding habits, method of travel, reading sign, and familiarity with the general characteristics of whitetails help the bowhunter anticipate many of the things which occur in hunting. Knowing where to hunt at various times of the day may well spell the difference between success and failure. Observing game while afield and making mental notes for future reference is the best classroom any hunter can attend.

Hunter movement at the wrong time has lost many a trophy head even though the deer has been "sweated" into shooting range. The importance of remaining motionless while on a stand should be repeatedly stressed to beginners; only those experienced can testify how vitally important this is.

If you ever closely examine the eye of a whitetail you will notice that its outer scanning surface protrudes more than in the case of the human eye. It is located farther away from the skull and this, too, makes it possible for the whitetail to better see over a wider range. Since the whitetail lacks the ability to move its eyes to either side in the same way as humans, nature has endowed it with extra-keen side vision. This enables it to detect movements over a wide range to the side, front, and to the rear of its seemingly fixed gaze. So the whitetail does not necessarily have to have his head turned in your direction to see some movement on your part. To illustrate this point, consider the following example of how these senses or abilities are present in man but seem never to be developed to fullest use.

Of his several perceptive senses the hunter employs three especially in pursuit of game. These are his senses of smell, sight, and hearing. Each has an important use in hunting whether it be in stalking, while posted as a watcher, in tracking wounded game or in actual shooting.

The approach of game can be detected by the alarming chatter of the squirrel as he watches from the safety of a tree after having been chased away from a favorite feeding area. The rasping call of the blue jay or whiskey jack will denote something intruding in your area. If you are hunting at the time of the year when rutting is in progress, the soft muted blatt, sounding very much like a young lamb, may mean a doe standing nearby. She may be calling a buck or she may be calling her fawn of last spring, which is still running with her. The snort of the alarmed deer does not always mean its departure but may merely mean a clearing of the nostrils as it searches the air currents for more definite danger scents.

The coughing call of a deer usually is a signal that it has detected and is telling others of danger. The sharp whistle-like noise made by deer usually is from a buck, suddenly startled by danger.

The approach of game can usually be detected by its traveling noise. When you are stationed on watch and quiet, these noises, never usually heard in stalking, become quite discernible to the normal human ear.

Over years of hunting with both rifle and the bow I believe I have detected the presence of more game by ear than by sight or smell. Often I was therefore ready to shoot before actually sighting the game. Many a squirrel, for example, has alerted me minutes before I could see a bushy tail.

Long periods of time spent on a watch in a quiet forest tend to improve an individual's hearing. We depend so much on combinations of sound in our routine life that its absence may unconsciously cause us to listen harder in order to break what seems to us to be a not only unusual but also undesirable state. It is well to remember that every wild animal has a higher developed sense of hearing than we humans. Since the whitetail's life depends on an acute hearing, he will employ it to his fullest ability. Govern your movements accordingly and realize that every noise and sound you make convey danger signals to your quarry before it either sights or scents you.

Most hunters have at some time or another been posted on watch in isolated forest spots. The longer you remain motionless while watching, the keener your eyes become. Since your vision is confined to very few, if any, moving objects, your eyes seem somehow to sharpen decidedly, and vision seems to increase both in range and ability to penetrate the shadows. Thus, you often feel able to detect movements out of the corner of your eyes and without turning your head. But as you detect slight movements to your right or left (only momentarily noticed), you must turn your head in the direction in which you detected that movement in order to check.

Usually it will be a small bird or squirrel, or perhaps a chipmunk that scurries about in search of food. But at times that movement may be the flick of a tail or that of a feeding deer. This is a result of employing your complete power of vision. Actually, you are sharpening your ocular ability while the rest of your body is relaxed, thus you permit complete concentration on visual perception.

We don't do this too often in our everyday life, but practice will help at home as well as in the forest. If a quiet spot is available such as a secluded garden or back yard where distracting sounds and objects will not conflict, you can practice and experiment with improving your visual perception. Relax on a chair or on the lawn, concentrate your thought to a slow roving gaze and scan the area around you very thoroughly. After some practice you find increased ability to detect movements to your left or right, movements outside your accustomed angle of vision. And, you needn't turn your head in the direction of movements. Try it. This leads to the final phase, *pick a spot to hit.*

Many hunters at some time or other are the victim of the common habit of aiming for the whole deer instead of picking a spot to hit. While the rifle hunter may in some cases still make a hit when aiming in this manner, the bowhunter usually finds himself faced with a miss.

Thinking back to the basics of good bowmanship one remembers that concentrating on the pimple is required to get all the arrows in the five ring. The same applies when drawing an arrow on a deer.

Placing an imaginary spot in the vital area you must hit for a kill is necessary. Concentrating on that spot only will avoid overshooting. Once you have placed this imaginary spot, never let your gaze wander from that part of the body until your arrow has reached its target.

14

Practicing Unorthodox Positions

AFTER emerging from the novice class, the successful bowhunter must concentrate less on shooting form and more on practicing every unorthodox position he can think of. For only thus can he ready himself for the complex shots that will present themselves in hunting and expect to be able to hunt with successful results.

Let no one misinterpret my views as deemphasizing the need for proper basic archery training. It is vitally important that the reader realize that I think of him as having progressed to the category of an advanced archer when I stress the need for training in unorthodox positions of shooting.

Proper basic training supervised by qualified archers is a must for the beginner. It is imperative that the budding bowhunter learn all the fundamentals properly as he becomes familiar with his weapons. Proper release, proper anchor point, proper bow holding, follow through after the shot, etc., are vitally necessary to condition the archer for hunting. Just as the rifleman must learn how to align his sights properly, squeeze the trigger and assume the proper hold in basic training, so too the archer must adapt himself first to the fundamentals.

After a recognized amount of skill is developed through shooting on the target course during which habits are developed in proper shooting form, the archer leaves the novice class.

By then he has developed a degree of accuracy through consistent practice and application of the proper fundamentals. Now the archer holds his bow properly, releases smoothly, and anchors properly. And unconsciously, he has developed an instinctive judgment of distance while in the process of learning to handle the bow. His score has improved considerably since he shot his first arrow at a target, and he finds now that further improvements are possible only through close personal observation while practicing consistently.

If he now desires to hunt with the bow, he may add to what he has already developed, namely the diversified shooting ability that hunting demands. With proper indoctrination in bow shooting now completed he can step into this new phase without harming his skill. But it should be clearly understood that a beginner should not entertain the thought of taking up unorthodox positions of shooting until he has first attained a fair degree of skill and familiarity with his weapon through conventional training and practice.

Again, for the sake of comparison, the rifleman does not undertake the task of trying to hit running targets until he has become fairly skillful in hitting a stationary target. Through learning to shoot from prone, sitting, kneeling, and offhand positions he has developed an adeptness with his weapon and at least a fair degree of accuracy. Now he is ready to advance to the more complicated and tougher targets, which demand faster timing and shooting.

After the archer can go around a twenty-eight target field course using no more than eight arrows and making a score of no less than one hundred and fifty, and after he has had at least one year of bowshooting experience, he is ready for advanced hunting training. Until then, he should walk slowly, learning properly as he goes. A poor beginning through lack of training in the fundamentals of archery will never allow the necessary background for successful bowhunting to develop.

There are many archery abilities that must be developed by the individual for himself. But, as in every sport, basic form and proper procedure are stepping stones to advanced skill. Without a thorough knowledge of the limitations and capabilities of the weapon, it would be a waste of time to undertake advanced training in unorthodox hunting positions.

Good books on how to learn to shoot the bow and advice from experienced archers should have a place in every beginner's routine.

The roving-type of practice shooting is the most beneficial method of conditioning the bowhunter. With this method one target butt or big-game target can be used. The shooter keeps moving about within range of the target making shots from various angles and distances as well as from varied positions. For example, one shot is made from a stooped position at twenty yards at an angle for forty-five degrees to the target. A second shot is released at thirty yards from a kneeling position direct broadside to the target. The next shot is made at a different angle and distance as you keep moving around the target; using a different shooting stance each time, make each shot from an entirely different position, angle, and distance. Where possible, place the target in the center of the shooting area and work around it. This kind of practice is only to be done in an area where all safety considerations permit. Location, terrain, and surrounding properties must be considered in determining the safety of such an arrangement. Where children are present in areas immediately adjoining, utmost safety precautions must be observed at all times. In some cases it will be necessary to shoot from one side only, placing your target along some blind side of the area unapproachable to pedestrians. Warning signs placed around the perimeter of the shooting area will caution grownups but are not an adequate protection for children. The safest practice therefore is to avoid locating target shooting near children.

The archer must always be constantly watchful for persons who may wander within range of his shafts. Extremely long shots should be avoided; shafts that miss the butt are dangerous!

There are many variations of unorthodox shooting position for the bowhunter to practice such as step-outs to left and right, keeping one foot in normal stride, then stop but reverse your body at the waist, leaving the feet still in their forward-stride position. From this awkward position release your shot at a side angle to the target. Canting the bow to an abnormal degree on these shots is excellent practice. You can even go the limit and practice shots practically "upside down."

Sitting shots and shots from prone position should be practiced. Also a butt can be placed near a tree to provide some tree shooting practice. Get used to shooting through small openings of foliage and between branches and get into some unusual positions while practicing this. Keeping your balance at the same time is a problem that will also be overcome through such practice.

For the faster moving target-type of shooting, use rubber blunts on flying or rolling disks. This is excellent practice which gives you a chance to use old shafts and is highly helpful in improving your snapshot techniques. Aluminum-alloy disks, twelve inches in diameter are fine for this; they can be tossed into the air or rolled along the ground by a companion. The rolling disk is great practice for the rabbit hunter, while the flying disk helps sharpen the eye for both wing shots and running deer. Such shooting practice develops a keener eye, while timing and reflex coordination are also noticeably improved.

15

Big-Game Targets

FOR THE deer hunter a semi-dimensional target provides realistic shooting practice and a good sighting picture. Such a target can be made by several archers or a club's range committee. Methods of moving the target can vary from the motor driven to the hand-propelled system, depending on available funds and the mechanical abilities of the members.

A low-cost target of suitable proportions can be constructed as follows:

Material list

- Life-size pattern of deer (running or standing).
- Styrofoam planking (12 inches wide, 48 inches long, 2 inches thick)
- Lacquer thinner
- Rubber roller
- Wooden skewers or thin doweling
- Weldwood mastic or Elmer's glue
- Bricks or cinder blocks for weights
- Pruning saw or keyhole saw
- Wood rasp (coarse)
- Carpenter's blue chalk (cake or powder)
- Eight-ounce burlap material
- Rubber base paint

Lamination of the styrofoam planking is built up until the desired thickness is achieved for body depth. If this is to be a standing target, the pin stakes must be built in during the laminating phase. Or, if it is to be a running target, one used on a cable rig, build in the blocks at this phase. End-to-end pieces are then glued together using lacquer thinner applied with a rubber roller. Apply sparingly and quickly. Make the butt joints. Use wood skewers to pin together and remove later when dry. Stagger these butt joints on each layer of build-up similar to the staggering of brick joints on a wall.

Layers are glued together with Weldwood resin plastic glue or Elmer's glue as you laminate to required thickness. When enough

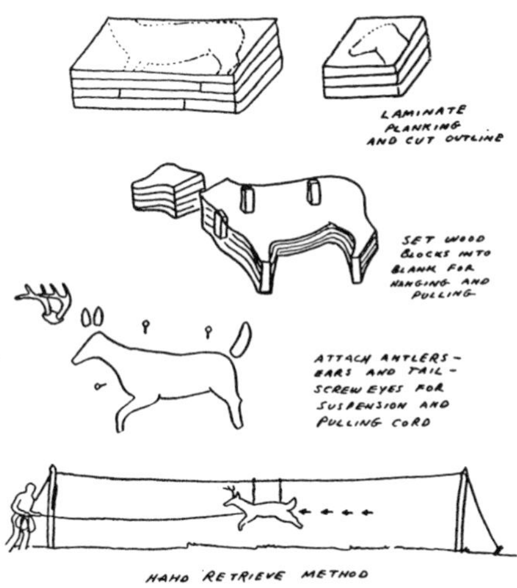

layers are built up to proper thickness, lay on a flat surface or floor. Place weights on top until dry. Use the bricks or cinder blocks for weights.

The shaping takes place next. Remove all excess material first with the pruning or keyhole saw. Then use the coarse wood rasp for final shaping. But here caution is advised; the styrofoam will cut like butter! Blanks for the ears and tail are next glued to the body in their proper places. Here again, use skewers to hold them in place. Remove the skewers when the parts are dry.

If a lifelike effect is desired, a set of antlers can be attached. The antlers must have the skull plate still attached. By coating the bottom side of the skull plate with carpenter's chalk you first make an impression on the styrofoam by pressing the plate in place. Then remove enough of the styrofoam to provide a proper bedding for the skull plate (about three-eighths inch in depth); then hold the plate in place against the head and mark and drill mounting holes (four inches deep) into the styrofoam. Attach permanently with wooden doweling and glue. Allow the dowels to protrude above the skull plate, trim after they are dry and properly set.

Last is the application of burlap sheathing to the form. Two layers are applied. A thin latex-base adhesive paint is used and this will be the most messy part of the job. Allow the first layer to dry thoroughly overnight, then apply a second layer in the same manner as the first. After this the finished form should be painted a lifelike brown with white at the throat, muzzle, and eyes. Nostrils and eyes may be painted black depending on the artistic inclinations of the target makers.

Note: For the standing-type target, build in the pin stakes during the laminating process. For a running target to be used on a cable rig, two wood blocks are installed in the top of the body during the laminating phase. See accompanying drawings for locations.

When completed, you have a target that will take quite a bit of pounding before it will start breaking down. For example, using field tips, the target should be good for at least several thousand shots in any one given area. Then when breakdown occurs, the affected area can be cut out and replaced with a new piece of material. The amount of shots the form will take is determined to a great extent by the strength of the outer sheathing of burlap. This, after all, is the retaining agent for the inner styrofoam core. Running targets will hold up longer than the standing type, since hits are apt to be more evenly distributed on the body.

Field-tipped wooden shafts or aluminum target shafts will penetrate and stick in these targets with bow weights ranging from twenty pounds and up. Withdrawal of shafts from the side of entrance is easy. Very few shafts will pass through the target's far side. If they do, it will be usually only a matter of a few inches.

The next target construction problem is to develop running gear, if a moving target is desired. The most inexpensive and simple way is to make a hand-propelled arrangement.

Material List

75 feet of steel stranded cable, 3/16th inch (aircraft control cable is excellent)
2 awning-type sheave pulleys
1 screen-door type coil spring
150-foot chalk line
2 sheets, sheathing-grade plywood, 4 x 8 feet, ¾-inch thick
2 sheets, Homosote board, 4 x 8 feet, 1-inch thick

If two trees or poles about 75 feet apart are available in the location where the target is to be placed, the cable is strung between these uprights. If uprights must be installed, the poles should be no less than four by fours, imbedded to at least a minimum of three feet. Tie-back braces of two by fours should be attached to each upright to counteract the inward pull of the cable.

Thread the two sheave-type awning pulleys on the cable before you span between the uprights. One end can be attached by wrapping while the other end should have a turnbuckle as

a means of removing all slack and making the cable taut.

Take the screen-door coil spring and cut in halves of equal length. Bend a hook in each end of the pieces using the coil wire for this purpose. Attach one end to each pulley (these hooks can be bent shut permanently). The other ends of the springs are attached to the deer target and the cable. (Here the hooks should be kept open for removal and switching.) The chalk line is attached to the target for moving it back and forth on the cable. By pulling in a jerky method with starts and stops you can produce a bobbing target effect. This is when the screen-door coil springs do their work.

The plywood sheets with an overlay of Homosote are erected at each end of the cable run to provide a shield for the operators of the target. The combined total thickness of one and three-fourths inches of material will stop shafts without fear of their penetration. The Homosote cushions and reduces the velocity of the shaft while the plywood furnishes the stopping resistance. Erect these protective shields with the eight-foot sides as the upright height and the four-foot ends as the base width. Scrap lumber is usually used in constructing the uprights to hold shields in position. In general, these shields will shuck off any target shaft shot from ranges of fifty yards. The firing line should be no less than this distance in order to conserve the target for use over a long period.

A very inexpensive and effective target can also be made in semi-dimensional form as follows:

Material List

Corrugated cardboard, in pieces 4 x 5 feet
Weldwood glue
Life-size pattern or sketch, on cardboard when laminated

Working for a total final thickness of no less than six inches, laminate the corrugated cardboard in layers using sufficient glue between each piece. When completed, place weights on top and let the target rest until dry.

Cut to shape along tracings of the bodyline pattern. During lamination, provide some means of attachment such as wooden pieces in proper positions for screw eyes at top of the back line. Or, if the target is to be stationary type, insert two, wooden, two-by-two extensions down through the legs. Point them to install the target in the ground.

If this target is desired to use as a running target, it can be attached and used by means of the same simple rig as mentioned for the other target.

16

Field Dressing

DEER field dressing methods have been discussed many times for the hunter's benefit in various articles and manuals. It would seem that with the many instructive and helpful leaflets that have been printed by game departments and sporting equipment manufacturers no hunter could possibly be anything but a first-class field-dresser. But, observing the mutilated and neglected game meat that leaves the forests each year, it seems to me that there still must be many who need help in this phase of hunting.

I have seen deer in which the entire body cavity was left badly smeared with stomach contents or waste matter from the large intestine. I have checked deer with lungs still in the chest cavity after hanging on the camp rail for days. One such deer when opened was quite ripe, having a good amount of accumulated blood that had congealed and soured, tainting the meat. Another common occurrence is to note the windpipe and gullet still left in deer, even after they are home and awaiting butchering.

I shall never forget one deer in particular as long as I do any hunting. It was shot by a veteran of some twenty-five odd years of hunting experience. Supposedly an expert in the eyes of his companions, his ways were accepted as proper without question. But his only real qualifications as an expert lay in his years of hunting, plus a record of having shot better than a dozen deer. A nice guy at heart, he meant well without a doubt; but he had never learned the proper way of taking care of his deer.

Unfortunately, this is the case with so many of the so-called "old timers." Too often, some of them know very little about the proper handling of their deer. They rely more upon extreme cold temperatures to hold their meat until they get it home. The sad part is that many inexperienced hunters try to learn from the "old timers" in such camps and are started out wrong. Hence they frequently end up taking home venison that will not be enjoyed by anyone. Instead it often winds up as dog food.

I happened to be hunting as a guest in the same camp with this hunter one year. It was during a rifle season for bucks only. One morning the "old timer" shot a small five-pointer along a little creek. Being close by, I happened to come upon him as he started field-dressing the buck. So I stood back to watch the "master" work, and what I saw took all my will power to keep myself from butting in. But, since he was many years my senior, I kept my lips buttoned. He gave no regard to bursting the bladder and spilling the urine into the body cavity, nor did he remove the stomach and intestines with care. Instead, they were literally torn out, leaving quite an untidy mess inside. The chest cavity was not touched. The diaphragm, together with the heart and lungs, were left intact. When he rose and put his knife away, he grabbed the buck by the hind-legs and dragged it over to the creek and started washing the steaming deer's body cavity with ice-cold mountain water. After doing this, he took a rope out of his pocket, wrapped it around the flanks, and bound the carcass opening until it was sealed tightly. I finally gave him a hand dragging his buck back to camp.

Upon reaching camp, this buck was hung on the porch by the hind legs and thus left for the next four days. During this time the mid-day temperatures hit the sixties and the buck had all of the benefits of several days' basking in afternoon sun. When we left for home at the end of the week's hunt, one of the boys removed the rope which had kept the body opening sealed and the stench nearly took off his hat! But the responsible veteran hunter assured everyone that this would not have anything to do with edibility of the meat!

Not having connected during my week of hunting, I was invited to pick up a share of the venison when they butchered it later at home. I refused with the polite excuse that I just did not care for venison at all, anytime. Later I learned that the entire carcass was sour and unfit to eat, a condition I had figured was inevitable.

To properly field dress a deer is to prepare the carcass for future human consumption, and it includes removal of all possible causes of spoilage from your game. If this is done sensibly, at least half the chance of enjoying sweet venison is already in your favor before your deer reaches camp. All internal organs must be removed completely, the hunter taking care that none of the contents is dropped or smeared inside the body cavity during removal.

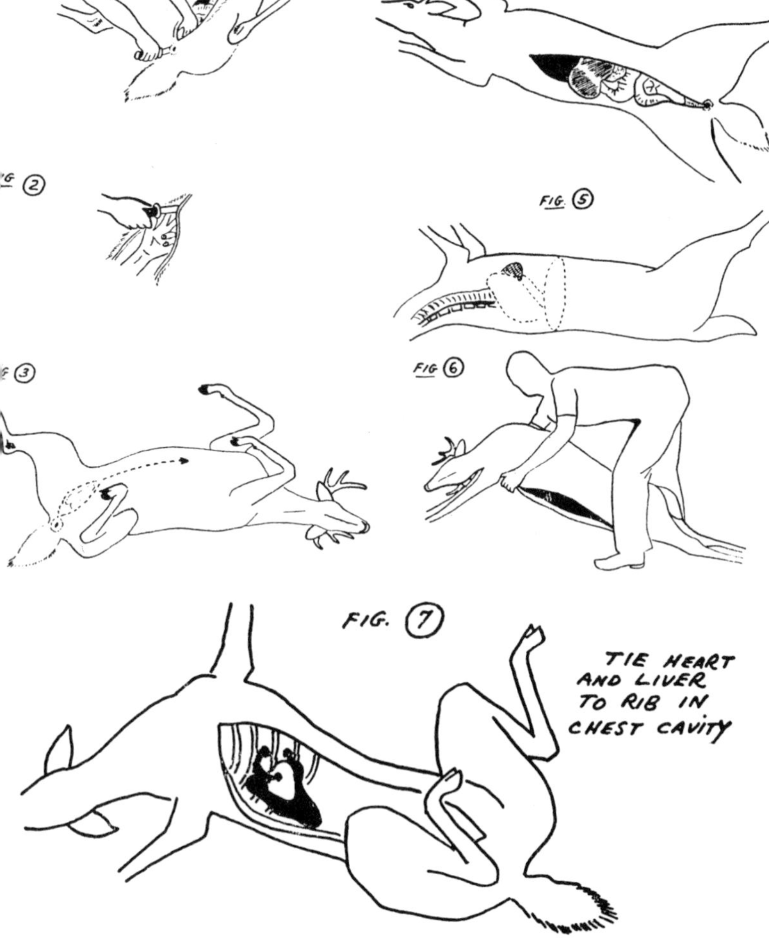

1/ Make circular cut around anus and genitals, freeing them so they can be drawn into body cavity still attached to lower intestine. Begin cut to side of anus. 2/ Use two fingers of free hand to guide knife and prevent cutting inner organs. Then work knife up slowly towards chest. 3/ Continue incision past each side of genitals, then form one cut up to chest bone (see dotted line). Discard reproductive organs; free liver and save. 4/ Roll deer on side, reach in and with a firm tug roll out the stomach and intestines. 5/ Roll deer on its back. Cut through diaphragm and remove heart, lungs, and windpipe from chest cavity. Save heart. 6/ Roll deer over on its belly; straddle it, grasping deer behind front legs under chest. Lift and shake carcass until well drained of blood. 7/ Move carcass to clean spot; pierce holes in heart and liver and at each side of a rib. Heart and liver properly tied to a rib with strong cord will not be lost during transport with carcass to camp.

17

Packing and Camp Handling Your Venison

WHENEVER conditions permit and help is available, let your deer cool and stiffen before moving in order to assure tender and sweet meat.

Remember, if you must drag your deer, do so while the carcass is still warm because cold meat bruises easily. Drag the deer by the head and *with* the grain of the hair for easier going. This way less dirt will accumulate inside the carcass than if it is dragged against the grain of the hair. Don't let a few leaves or particles of brush worry you if they should work their way into the body cavity during the trip. This minor forest debris will not harm the meat, and it can readily be removed when you get the carcass back to camp.

Dragging your deer, if a buck, by the method of attaching the ends of your rope to its antlers and using a loop around your waist is a practice that bears watching. In downhill terrain with a good sliding snow, that buck may hit you from behind when you stop for a breather or at some obstacle. Once I saw one hunter actually get butted off the edge of a steep slide which he was descending. He came upon the slide unexpectedly, hence stopped abruptly, but the buck behind him didn't! Luckily the hunter wasn't hurt, but keep in mind that the sharp tines of antlers can possibly jab your legs or back badly in such an instance.

During the bowhunting season, an archer can pack his deer out on his back without fear of having it shot off his shoulders in contrast with the hazards faced by hunters who must take out their deer in other seasons. The average man can pack a hundred-pound field-dressed deer if the distance is not too far. If the deer is a buck, be sure the head is secured to prevent its bobbing back and forth with your every stride. If you use the

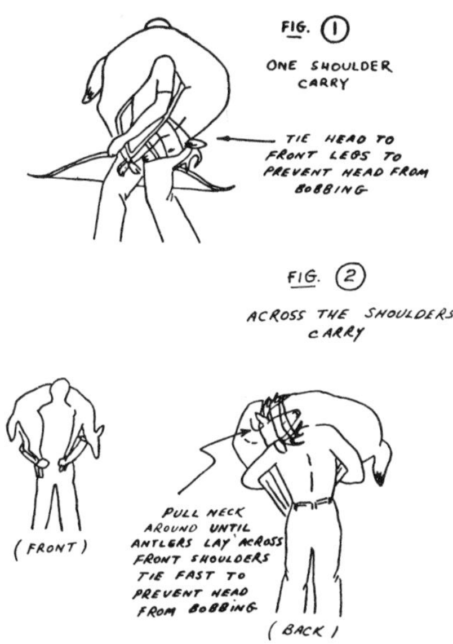

"one-shoulder carry," tie the antlers to the front leg and carry your deer hind-end first.

In case companions are with you, the deer can be carried by means of the pole-carry. This is a very good method if the portage distance is longer than usual. Select a tree about ten to twelve feet tall and about three to four inches in diameter. Usually you can find a suitable one without desecrating the forest. Cut and trim it. Be sure to test it for strength by flexing it enough to assure that it can support the weight of a deer bobbing along. The pole is then passed between the front and back legs of the deer carcass.

Starting at the deer's muzzle, lash the head and neck to the pole, then cross the front legs and lash them to the pole. Continue the rope around the body and pole to the hind-legs. These are also cross-lashed around the pole, similar to fastening the front quarters. When completed, the carcass will be as parallel with the carrying pole as possible and lashed securely to prevent shifting. A tight lashing job prevents excessive weaving or bobbing of the carcass being carried. But in this position the legs of the deer stick straight up and sometimes pose a problem striking against overhead branches. Therefore I always knuckle my deer before packing in this fashion, and this eliminates the problem.

Simply cut the legs off at the carpals (or wrist joint) of the front legs and slightly below the tarsus (or ankle joint) of the hind legs. *Caution:* The cut of the hind leg must be made below the tarsus joint so that the main tendon of the hock is intact for hanging the carcass in later butchering and skinning.

If the hunter desires to use the deer's feet in taxidermy later, they can be bundled to carry out as a separate package. A folded jacket placed on the pole shoulder will serve well as a pad during the trek back to camp. The rear man should match the stride of the leading packer. By the packers falling in step, their strides will tend to produce less cargo bobbing. The cargo

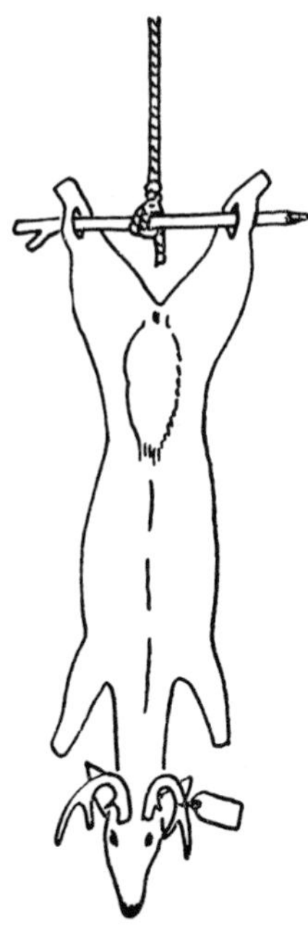

weaving resulting from uneven strides by the packers has the effect of adding to the burden and may actually throw the carrying men off balance. Where a group of hunters are together and take turns with the carry, a long distance can be covered without too much difficulty and before they realize it.

After your deer has been taken, field dressed, and brought into camp, a most important part of the hunt involves your care of the carcass. If properly handled, you will have some of the most tasty portions of venison possible for real "out of this world" eating pleasure. But if improperly handled, you will have only sour and tainted meat, definitely containing that "wild taste" so often associated with venison or other big-game meats. And too often when venison or other big game is served at the dining room table, the words are heard, "Oh, I don't care for any, thank you. I don't like the wild taste." I have known many men who hunt each deer season but will not eat any of their game. It is a shame, indeed, that such fine food is passed up by so many, mostly because of carelessness by hunters in handling the carcasses.

In most areas the bow season comes at a time of the year when average temperatures are bound to be in the mild margin, often running even into the seventies during mid-day. This means that two problems arise in connection with the bowhunter's deer. The first of these is the warm temperature, which means problems in keeping the carcass from spoiling. The second problem is insects, with the blow fly as the main nuisance.

In order to keep his venison sweet, properly cooled, and protected, the bowhunter must take certain precautions. Then, if properly handled, his venison will be as edible and tasty as any he ever ate.

After having reached camp with his deer, the first and most important step he must take is to remove the hide or skin from the carcass as soon as possible, preferably within three hours of the kill. Body heat trapped between the skin and the meat of the carcass cannot otherwise dissipate fast enough and the venison will taint and sour speedily in the warm temperatures. Air cooling is the proper method of getting the body heat out of the carcass without damaging the taste and quality of the meat. Cooling must be promoted on the outer surface of the carcass as effectively as within. For this reason the hide covering all edible portions must be removed in order to assure proper meat cooling.

Skinning will be much easier when the body and skin still retain some body heat, but it is a difficult operation with a carcass that has hung in cold temperatures for several days.

A shady spot should be selected for hanging the deer, and the carcass then suspended by the head and high enough to prevent damage from stray dogs, skunks, or other animals. Deer should never be hung by the hind quarters because then the blood collects in the forward part of the chest cavity where it will sour the meat. By suspending the carcass by the head, the blood will drain out through the body opening and in this way it cannot pool or congeal to damage the meat. Skinning should extend as far as the head or upper part of the neck. Leave the skin attached to the carcass at this point. It can now be gathered, bundled, and tied to the suspending lines or the rack of the head. Then later when transporting the deer home, the hide can be unrolled and used as a protective covering for the carcass.

If the head is to be mounted for a trophy, skinning in this manner will not ruin the cape for taxidermy work; that is, with one exception. If a full-shoulder mount is wanted, the skinning must include about ten inches of the front legs with the main hide. Arrange this by cutting carefully down the back center of the front legs to the ten-inch mark. At this point make a circling cut around the leg to separate this portion from that on the rest of the leg. Consider all the hide above this circling cut as a part of the main hide. The back cut along the center of the neck or cape can be made after your deer is at home and the head separated from the carcass. Assuming you are following this and since by now you will have skinned down to a point near the ears, all as one piece, merely turn the hair side of the hide out and let your taxidermist cut whatever amount of cape he needs from the entire hide. He will then make the cut necessary along the back of the neck precisely as he needs for his mounting purposes. (See illustrations at chapter end.)

After the hide has been removed but before you start the task of "caping out" the head, if desired, the carcass should be covered by a cheesecloth sack or some form of commercial big-game bag. The material to be used for covering must be of a porous nature similar to cheesecloth, permitting free circulation of air and at the same time preventing insects from getting to the meat. This eliminates the blow-fly from his dirty work of laying eggs in the meat, eggs which later hatch into the small maggots that cause its complete deterioration.

As the carcass hangs and air cools naturally, it may turn a darker color on the outside evolving a glazed shell as the outer surface dries a bit. This is nothing to become alarmed about; it is a natural reaction to the air, in fact, an indication that all is well. However, if you intend to age your meat before freeze-storing it upon getting home, watch this glazed outer shell for indications of its getting slick or wet. When and if this condition shows, place the carcass under refrigeration at once. Aging should be permitted only for a maximum period of one week before freezing and storing the meat. I advise that you consult someone experienced along these lines if you feel your deer should be aged instead of chancing the job on your own. After handling the first one, you will, of course, probably be able to take care of others yourself; but don't gamble on aging that first deer without experienced advice.

Should the hunter wish to have the head mounted and if the weather is extremely warm, he is going to have to promptly skin out the head to prevent slippage of the hair. The main thing is to allow ample cape with which the taxidermist can work.

Skinning out a head is not as tough a job as it sounds, but it does require patience and it means taking your time. I have successfully skinned out several heads, and I am sure you can do likewise. The tools needed are a good skinning knife plus a medium-sized screwdriver. The screwdriver comes in handy at such places as around the eyes and nostrils. Exercise care while cutting away adhesions so your knife does not cut through the skin. After completely removing the skin from the skull, the antlers are cut out with a saw. However, be sure to leave a sizeable skull base plate attached to the antlers. The taxidermist will cut this down to his desired size.

The cape must now be salted down very generously to absorb all the wetness from the inner skin surfaces. The cape should then rest flat overnight, then all the salt is removed on the following morning, a generous fresh layer applied again. By this time most of the moisture will have been absorbed by the first salting. The cape can now be propped or hung to drain any remaining moisture. After another six to eight hours, this coat of salt is also removed. Then spread the cape out flat and again generously salt it, roll it, and stand it up on end until you are ready to leave for home. Figure on plenty of salt for the job, no less than ten pounds per head. Table salt will do the job better than a coarser variety. Be sure to pack plenty of salt in the ears, working it well inside, for here is where slippage is the most likely. And keep in mind that salt will never harm the hair side of your cape.

We have assumed that the deer was field dressed in the proper manner before it was hung, skinned, and allowed to cool. All parts of the carcass have undergone a thorough cleaning as prescribed for proper field-dressing. The lungs, heart, windpipe, and gullet have been properly removed and all blood drained completely. The inner cavity has been wiped clean with a cloth. The original carcass opening has been extended from the sternum bone in front of the chest to the pelvic bone between the hind-legs, and small sticks have been used to prop open the carcass for complete cooling.

The next and final important step in assuring yourself delicious venison is to get your deer home as soon as possible, cut it into proper portions, and place it under refrigeration. Start by keeping the deer *off* the front fender or hood of your car where engine heat and fumes may permeate the meat. Transport the deer either on top of your car or in the trunk; if in the trunk, leave the lid somewhat ajar to provide for adequate air circulation.

Invariably questions will arise concerning your deer's live weight. This no longer need be the subject of pure conjecture or speculation, although in practically every case the hunter brings his deer home minus that part of its weight removed in field-dressing. Nevertheless, the following table will give you an accurate measure of your deer's live weight, with no guessing involved. The left-hand column lists field-dressed weights in ten-pound graduations. Find your deer's present weight in this column. A corresponding figure in the right column will tell you the deer's live weight. For example, reference to the chart shows that a deer that weighed one hundred-ten pounds field-dressed (internal organs including heart, liver, and lungs removed), weighed one hundred and forty pounds (see right-hand column).

Dressed Weight	*Live Weight*	*Dressed Weight*	*Live Weight*
40	55	130	165
50	65	140	185
60	80	150	190
70	90	160	205
80	105	170	215
90	115	180	230
100	130	190	240
110	140	200	255
120	155		

Before the carcass is split, measure the girth just front of the back legs. Then using the following table, determine the approximate weight of your deer.

Girth in Inches	*Pounds Hog Dressed*	*Girth in Inches*	*Pounds Hog Dressed*
29	60	38	115
30	65	39	125
31	70	40	135
32	75	41	145
33	80	42	160
34	85	43	175
35	90	44	190
36	95	45	210
37	105	46	230

The above table is carried by Game Protector Ken Hess, Lehigh County, Pennsylvania. He has found it a big help in determining the weight of deer killed on the highways. Checking the figures against actual weighing of such deer, he has determined the table to be accurate within three pounds on an average.

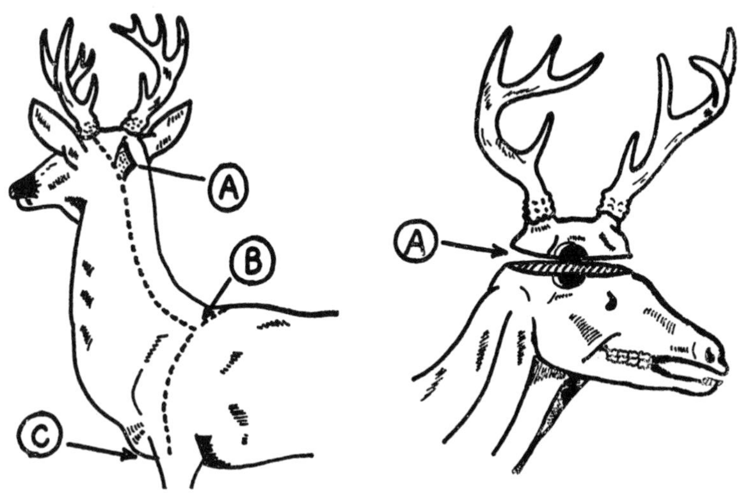

Caping Cuts

(Left) Starting at the base of each antler, on the upper back side, a vee cut is made with the two cuts meeting at point (A) and then continuing down the top of the neck as shown with the dotted line to point (B). Here the cut is brought around the front shoulders with the circling cut across the front of the leg (C). If a full shoulder mount is desired, the circling cut (C) should be on the inner side of the front leg and well back on the shoulders.

(Right) Skull Cut. After the cape has been completely removed from the head of the deer a meat or hacksaw is used to make cut (A) separating the horn plate from the skull. This cut should be through the center of the eye sockets with care being taken to make a straight cut. The result will be ample horn plate to keep the antlers intact and provide sufficient bone to fasten to the form when being mounted.

18

Butchering Your Deer

BACK HOME from a successful hunt, the task of butchering a deer carcass is quite simple. Follow a procedure similar to that used in cutting any other edible animal correctly. Certain cuts will provide roasts of different types while other parts of the carcass are more suitable for use as stewing meats or for ground meat. Steaks, likewise, are cut out of certain parts of the carcass to assure tenderness and tastiness. By referring to the following chart which shows each part of the carcass and the cuts obtained, the hunter who is butchering his first deer will wind up with choice cuts for his table.

The tools needed for a good job are a meat saw and several sharp meat-cutting knives, and a cleaver or small camp axe. You will also need a suitable table to work on and containers in which to place the cuts until butchering is completed.

A gambrel bar is used to hang a deer and facilitate its cutting into two sides or halves. Such a bar can be homemade from several materials and serve well for the job intended. For example, an old broom-handle, 36-inches long, will work fine, as long as the ties to the overhead anchor point are securely attached to each end of the handle. Just one tie in the center is likely to put too much strain on the handle, especially if you have a fairly heavy deer. By drilling holes through the handle six inches from each end, you can stick ten-penny nails through to act as stops. This will keep the hind-legs spread during sawing, especially when you saw along the spine.

Be sure that the overhead point from which you hang your deer is strong enough to withstand the strain while you work on the carcass. A joist will do, if indoors, or a strong branch will serve, if outside.

Hang your carcass by the hind hocks. Space the legs apart as far as possible to secure a splitting action when you saw down the center of the backbone separating the two sides. This

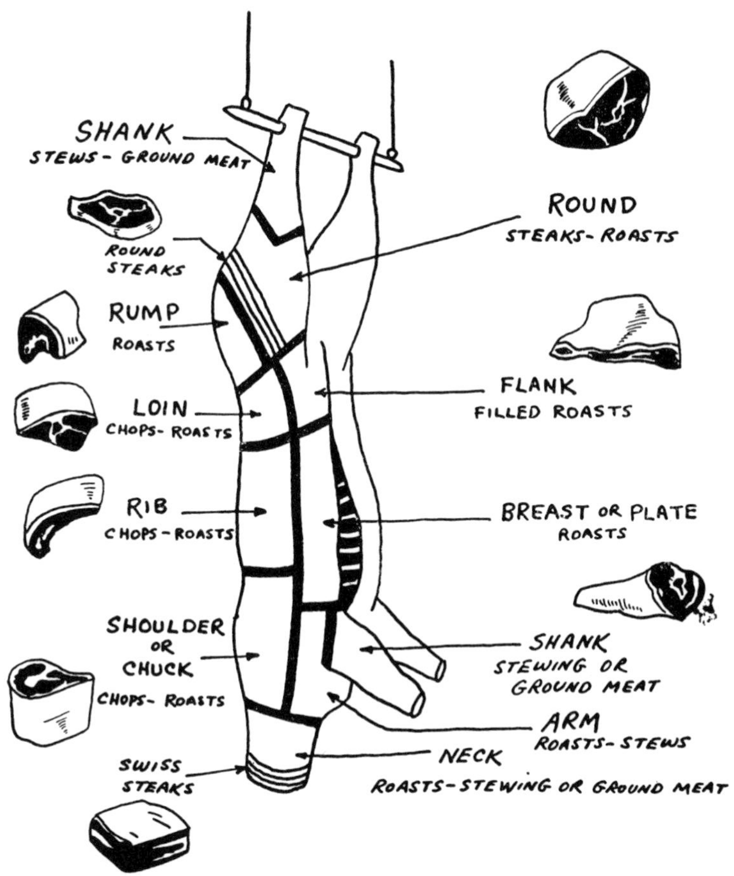

is done with the meat saw from start to finish. Start sawing at the tail and end up at the neck. While one side is left hanging, the other can be then laid out on the table as you prepare to make the various cuts.

After your butchering job is complete the cuts are wrapped in freezer paper and marked. Later when you dig out a roast or steak you will enjoy some real eating. You have done everything necessary to assure yourself of some good venison.

19

Venison on the Table

VENISON is a meat of individual character but of high-quality taste. Fine-grained in texture, large portions such as roasts require an added basting agent when being prepared. Venison fat cannot be used in cooking, for it is far from tasty, containing a tarty tallow-like quality not desired in the kitchen. Therefore all the fat should be trimmed off very carefully and discarded. Since your final portions will be lean after such trimming, a basting agent should be employed to replace the natural fat agents for proper broiling or roasting.

Two tasty ways of serving venison are worth mentioning here, for I am sure those who try them will find them both a gourmet's delight. Instead of the conventional steak cuts, try cutting chips, as thin slices as possible. Fry these to a quick turn in a hot skillet using shortening or butter. This will require very little time because of the thin meat cuts. They will melt in your mouth as you experience a new taste in venison eating pleasure.

VENISON CHIPS (breaded) (Pennsylvania Dutch Style)

2 eggs
cracker crumbs
salt and pepper

Use chips sliced as thin as possible and in a quantity according to the number of people to be served. Soak them in salt water for two hours. Drain and rinse in clear water and dry on paper toweling. Tenderize and prepare to bread. Beat the two eggs thoroughly, then add salt and pepper and place the bread crumbs on a flat plate. Dip the chips into egg, then both sides in crumbs and repeat again. Place in a pan of hot Mazola oil, fry to a quick turn, and serve. If preferred, the chips can be made without breading; they are just about as tasty.

ROAST VENISON (Pennsylvania Dutch Style)

4 pound venison roast
2 stalks celery with leaves
1 cup of water
1 large onion sliced thick
salt and pepper
2 tablespoons extract of meat (such as Wilson's BV)

Soak roast in salt water for five hours. Rinse in clear water, peel off all thin membrane and dry with paper toweling. Place in roast pan, rubbing salt and pepper into the meat. Heat the cup of water to boiling and dissolve extract of meat in the water. Pour over roast, place celery and onion slices around roast. Cover and roast in moderate oven heat (350 degrees) for approximately three and one-half hours. Baste every half-hour with the drippings in the pan.

A four-pound roast may be more than two people will consume at a meal, but don't throw the leftover roast away or feed it to the pup, for you have the makings of the best barbecue you ever sank your teeth into.

Barbecued venison is another taste treat for the dinner table. It is a wonderful way of using leftover portions of a large roast served in a former meal. For my money, it is as tasty as the original roast in every way. Various recipes of barbecues can be used, each reflecting individual taste. Barbecued venison served on rolls makes for a real good "man-type" eating. For real eating pleasure try this:

VENISON BARBECUE (Pennsylvania Dutch Style)

1 cup catsup
1 quarter cup cider vinegar
1 teaspoon of A-1 Sauce
1 teaspoon salt
1 onion sliced thin

Shred or fine-cut the leftover venison roast. The above ingredients are for about one and one-half pounds of meat. Mix the ingredients into sauce, place in saucepan with shredded meat and simmer slowly for three-quarters of an hour. Serve on oven-toasted round buns.

In our "Pennsylvania Dutch" country we have a cold meat called simply "dried beef," made from a choice piece of beef loin. It is cured and smoked into a tasty delicacy. Venison, cured and smoked in the same manner by some competent butcher, will prove worth your trying.

Fresh venison sausage as well as ground venison for meat loaves are ideal ways of serving tasty dishes, to say nothing about the luscious "venison-burgers" served on toasted rolls.

Try different ways of preparing venison dishes and open new avenues in delightful eating pleasure for your family and guests.

Swiss Venison Steak (Pennsylvania Dutch Style)

1 can No. 1 whole tomatoes
salt and pepper
1 teaspoonful of Worcestershire Sauce
2 sliced onions
1 teaspoonful of extract of meat

Mix the ingredients together with the exception of the onions, for a Swiss sauce. Place steak pieces cut approximately one-inch thick into a pan of hot Mazola oil. Brown both sides, remove, and place in a shallow roast pan. Slice the onions over the meat and cover with sauce mixture. Place in an oven heated to 350 degrees and bake for one hour.

Hunter's Venison Stew (Pennsylvania Dutch Style)

3 pounds of venison cut into 1½-inch cubes
¾ cup of Mazola oil
12 small onions peeled and left whole
1 stalk of celery cut into thick pieces.
3 cups beef bouillon
4 carrots sliced thick
salt and pepper

Soak the venison cubes in salt water for two hours, drain, and rinse in clear water. Dry on paper toweling. Dredge the cubes in flour and place in a stew pan in hot oil. Brown all sides carefully and then pour off practically all the oil. Add the three cups of bouillon and the rest of the ingredients. Simmer until the meat is tender.

Hunter's Delight Venison Liver (Pennsylvania Dutch Style)

Remove all membrane and thin skin, then slice the liver to medium thickness. Soak in salt water for twenty-four hours prior to preparing. Drain and rinse in clear water and dry on paper toweling. Dredge pieces in flour seasoned with salt and pepper and fry to a quick turn in a pan of hot oil. Then smother the pan of liver with sliced onions and brown slowly, turning all the time. There is another way to cook liver. After it has been dipped in flour, fry it a long time at low heat in a covered pan.

Hunter's Choice Venison Heart (Pennsylvania Dutch Style)

Carefully removing all the outer membrane, and the remaining artery by cutting down the center of the heart, the inner parts of the ventricles are rinsed, and the entire heart is placed in water with a pinch of salt. After the heart is thoroughly cooked, remove and rinse under cold water, set aside and allow to become cold.

When cold, slice to desired thickness to be served plain or pickled if desired.

For pickling mix the following ingredients:

1 cup warm water
½ cup vinegar
onion sliced thin
½ teaspoon salt
¼ teaspoon pepper

Place the sliced pieces of heart in the pickle mix and leave overnight. Serve the following day with the assurance of a tasty and unusual treat.

One of the favorite tricks that my wife and I sometimes employ is to have a meal for guests known to dislike wild meat because of its so-called "wild taste." Preparing venison in one of many tasty ways, my wife then serves it without identifying it. We both avoid any possible conversation which would give away our secret during the meal. Later, we ask the guests how they enjoyed the meal. Upon voicing their satisfaction, we ask them how they enjoyed the meat and then tell them they were eating venison. The reactions are amusing! Some will not believe it to be true while others simply stare in amazement. The usual reply is, "How did you prepare it to remove the wild taste?"

You can rest assured that if commercial packing houses handled beef and pork in the manner some sportsmen handle their deer, most of us would be vegetarians. Remember, when you tag and field-dress that deer next season it will have an invisible label attached, "Handle with Care!" If you do so, it will mean some wonderful eating for all who partake.

20

Pope and Young Competition

WITH so many of our present-day sportsmen accepting the challenge of bowhunting, many species of our North American big game have been taken by competent bowhunters. The enthusiasm for this method of hunting has spread into every hunting ground. Big-game animals that up until now were considered strictly rifle-class trophies are now listed among the world-record trophies taken by the bowhunter. And some of these animals are the envy of many seasoned big-game hunters who have been hunting with rifles for years.

Typical examples as to the bow's potency or "killing power" when in the hands of a skilled bowhunter are listed in the compilations of the new organization, The Pope and Young Club. Listed among the trophies are such powerful animals as the formidable polar bear and that brute of the browns, the Kodiak bear. The unpredictable and dangerous grizzly has also been recorded as well as many blacks. The elusive sheep ram is listed in two species as well as the tough Rocky Mountain goat. Many other species are found among the presently listed trophies such as caribou, moose, antelope, elk, and cougar. More record trophies by bowhunters undoubtedly will be added.

The leading animal on a nationwide basis taken by big-game bowhunters is still the deer. Four species are listed with the mule deer holding a slight edge over the whitetail. Next in line is the blacktail, and one trophy is listed as the Coues deer.

The Pope and Young Club was started back in 1957 to provide bowhunters with a system for records and awards patterned after the world-famous Boone and Crockett Club of New York. The first meeting was held in Grayling, Michigan, June 29, 1961.

The Boone and Crockett Club has given permission to use their well-established system of measuring trophy animals. Realizing that the bowhunter cannot be as selective as the hunter with a rifle, a lower minimum-point requirement has been set for each animal. This is done to provide maximum competition for the bowhunter.

The following are the Pope and Young minimum scoring points:

Whitetail Deer (Typical)	115
Whitetail Deer (Non-typical)	105-115
Mule Deer (Typical)	125
Mule Deer (Non-typical)	105-125
Columbian Blacktail Deer	75
Coues Deer	68
Yellowstone Elk	250
Roosevelt Elk	210
Mountain Caribou	265
Woodland Caribou	220
Barren Ground Caribou	265
Canada Moose	135
Alaska Moose	150
Wyoming Moose	115
Bighorn Sheep	130
White Sheep	120
Stone Sheep	120
Desert Sheep	115
Rocky Mountain Goat	35
Pronghorn Antelope	57
Alaska Brown Bear	20
Grizzly Bear	17
Black Bear	17
Polar Bear	15
Cougar	10
Jaguar	9

Pope and Young Competition is open to anyone. All animals taken with bow and arrow under the rules of fair chase during legal hunting seasons are eligible. If a preliminary entry meets the minimum requirements it can be entered in competition through having its measurements made by one of the Official Measurers. Forms and a list of the Official Measurers are available on request from the NFAA Secretary or the Pope and Young Records Committee, 19807 First Avenue South, Seattle 88, Washington.

All official entries are registered and judged. Winners are awarded special plaques, second and third places receive medals, and Honorable Mention certificates may be presented for any other trophies judged outstanding.

Awards will be made in each animal category unless insufficient entries are present in the given category to constitute real competition. Trophies once registered with the Committee for a specific competition are not eligible for any other future competition.

In conducting this competition, records of the finest trophies of North American big game taken with bow and arrow will become a reality for posterity. Competition covers the skulls, tusks, horns, and antlers of the listed animals.

It is the hope of the Committee to encourage bowhunters toward more qualitative hunting by awakening interest in outstanding North American big-game animals. It is the hope that all hunters will accept this new challenge of taking various types of trophy animals with the bow and arrow. The interest in conservation of the national wild life assets which our generation has inherited should be zealously protected by every outdoorsman and sportsman. If not, our future generations will only inherit a natural resource which we have wasted foolishly. As a means of fostering interest, sponsored competition with appropriate awards will be conducted annually.

Data secured from the heads and horns submitted will go into the archives as part of the file on records of North American big game. A current file of such statistics is an index, within limits, to localities most likely to produce trophy heads. This may disprove a common belief that modern trophies run smaller than those taken in "the good old days."

Regular membership requirements are the taking of three species of any adult animals listed. One of these must meet with the minimum-point requirements as listed with the Pope and Young Club. All trophies must be taken only in fair chase. Maximum membership is expected to be held to one-hundred regular members.

Associate membership will be held to a maximum of one hundred, chosen from those who by their general qualifications or allied interests in the Club recommend themselves for associate membership. As each associate member is accepted into the club he will be listed on a seniority basis for a future regular membership. This will be possible after he meets the regular membership requirements. Associate members will have no vote, but may be elected as one of several Vice-Presidents.

All big-game animals taken with bow and arrow which are entered for competition must be, as noted, taken in fair chase.

Excluded from means regarded as "fair chase" are the following instances or ways in which any big-game animal is killed:

(1) Helpless in, or because of deep snow.
(2) Helpless in water.
(3) Helpless on ice.
(4) Helpless in trap.
(5) While confined behind fences, as on game farms, etc.
(6) In defiance of game laws, or out of season.
(7) By jack-lighting or shining at night.
(8) From power vehicle or power boat.
(9) Any other method considered unsportsmanlike by the committee.

My membership in this organization is limited at present to that of an associate, but not for long if I can possibly help it. Having hunted only whitetails so far with the bow, I must hunt for and collect two other species. A Canadian bull moose is my next objective.

The competition and activities of this Club is a definite indicator of the future for bowhunting among big-game hunting sportsmen and proof positive regarding the effectiveness of the hunting arrow in the hands of a highly competent and skilled bowhunter.

Also there now exists challenges never before presented to the individual preferring big-game hunting. Can he develop sufficient skill in the face of the handicap of the limited range of the hunting bow to take an important species of animal in a class long considered only within the province of the rifleman? Can he apply this skill together with adeptness at stalking within close range of some of the largest and most dangerous big-game animals? Can he make the kill armed only with the hunting bow in the face of overwhelming odds and collect a trophy of enviable size? The demands in meeting such a challenge are greater than these offered in any other form of hunting today.

The personal satisfaction of collecting such trophies with a bow cannot be duplicated in any other form of hunting. Here is the opportunity for every outdoor-loving big-game hunter to justly earn his title. This is not for the big-game hunter who makes his kill from several hundred yards distance, a range used both as a safety precaution and as a vantage point. No, this is for a true hunter who through his knowledge of game is able to work his way within fifty yards of his animal, apply skill with his weapon, and make a clean kill.

21

Bowhunting in Various States

THE whitetail deer being the big-game animal sought by most bowhunters today, here are several states that offer some top hunting country. Several of the states now require that a non-resident bowhunter pass a written and practical shooting test before he can acquire the bowhunting permit or license. This is to be sure that the applicant is fully aware of the state's regulations and to be sure that he is familiar with his weapon. Applicants must be capable of shooting with a reasonable degree of accuracy and with regards to the safety of everyone afield.

Other states have certain minimum standards for equipment to be used such as a minimum bow weight, or power to cast an arrow a stipulated minimum distance such as one-hundred or one-hundred and fifty yards. The size of hunting heads, the number of cutting edges, and other details are regulated. In some states the use of wooden shafts only is specified.

Each year more thought and concern is being given to bowhunting by various conservation and game departments. This is consistent with the fact that the number of bowhunters is increasing from year to year at a steady pace. Game enforcement officers are beginning to learn about archery in order to understand the problems that confront the bowhunter. Also no doubt they must cope with some outlaw bowhunting. But the reports of the game departments contacted in this work seem to indicate a low percentage of game law violations by the bowhunters. In general, bowhunting has rated favorably and is generally accepted. It is here to stay. Among some of the states with established special archery seasons that offer good bowhunting for whitetails are New York, New Jersey, Michigan, Pennsylvania, and Wisconsin.

Wisconsin

Wisconsin had a total of eighty-nine days of bowhunting spread over two separate seasons during the course of one year. Its early season ran from September 17 to November 17 with a late season being from December 3 to December 31. Total reported kill was 1,091 deer.

Wisconsin claims credit for establishing the first bow-and-arrow season for deer in the United States. Since their first season in 1934, Wisconsin has had an annual season regularly except in 1935, in which year all deer seasons were closed.

Hunter success for gun hunters in deer hunting is rated at thirty percent in Wisconsin, but no more than five percent of the bowhunters connect. The sport offers top recreation though it results in a minimum harvest of game, an excellent use for a natural resource.

The following remarks concerning bowhunting have been released by the Wisconsin Conservation Department:

"There is little verification as to any considerable number of deer found dead later as the result of arrow wounds. Undoubtedly there are more crippled and wasted deer than are reported. Instances of these undesirable conditions are not as evident as the number of wasted deer resulting from other types of hunting.

"Non-resident bowmen have bagged about one-fourth of the total kill taken in the past seasons.

"Average killing distance figured to 25.7 yards, while six out of ten deer were shot while running. Average distance of recovery of deer after being hit was 162.7 yards.

"It follows that bowhunting is not a factor in game management in view of the insignificant kill records during the past seasons. The bowhunter's contribution to cropping deer in problem areas where browse is insufficient or where damage occurs is negligible. Probably an unlimited amount of bowhunting would have no appreciable effect on the harvest of deer where hard reduction is necessary.

"It is obvious that the records of past bow and arrow seasons have justified the liberal policies established by the State Conservation Commission."

The hot-spot county seems to be Juneau with a registered kill of 221 deer in these two seasons. Juneau is located in the west central area of the state. Vilas County placed second with a total kill of 137 for the same combined two seasons. Vilas is located in the northeast along the border of the state. In the northwest section, Bayfield runs third with a combined seasons' kill of 127.

The whitetails are not found in just a few sections of Wisconsin but are fairly well distributed throughout the area of the state's hunting lands. The highest kills were in areas where also the greatest concentration of bowhunters were found.

Wisconsin does not allow a strung bow in a car at any time. Heads used for hunting must be no less than seven-eighths of an inch; they may not be more than one and one-half inches in width. Pulling weight of bow must be thirty pounds or more for hunting. Metal big-game tags are used in Wisconsin. These are to be attached to the gambrel of either of the deer's hindlegs. Transporting deer between the time of kill and registration must be conducted in an open manner. If a deer is being transported in a car the trunk lid must be open to show enough of the deer to make it clear that it is being conveyed.

One deer of either sex can be taken with an archery permit. Cost of non-resident archery permit is ten dollars (for deer only). Sunday hunting is allowed. Hunting hours are listed in the regulations for each day of the season.

Wisconsin has rolling hills with fields bordered by timber stands of hardwoods and white birch, ridges and flats in the mountain areas with whitetails concentrated most around the agricultural areas.

For needed information covering a possible Wisconsin hunt contact the Wisconsin Conservation Department, Madison 1, Wisconsin.

New York

New York offers excellent whitetail hunting for the bowhunter. The Catskills and the Adirondacks are large mountainous areas abounding with deer. Counties bordering the Pennsylvania state line provide good whitetail bowhunting country, identical in terrain to the northern counties of Pennsylvania, which is prime deer country.

Season dates for archery hunting vary according to counties grouped as follows: Northern zone, Central and Western counties, Catskill and Eastern Counties.

In the Northern zone there is a fourteen-day season running from September 27 to October 11. This is a special season before the regular rifle season. Central and Western Counties and Catskills and Eastern Counties open November 3 and extend to November 17 for a special fourteen-day season before the regular rifle season. Westchester County opens November 15 and extends to December 31, with longbow hunting only, allowed.

Daily hunting hours are from 7 to 5, Sundays included. The non-resident bowhunting costs are twenty dollars. This includes a permit at ten dollars, plus a non-resident hunting license of ten dollars. Both permit and license are required. This allows the holder to take one deer of either sex, and one bear during the special bow and arrow period.

State regulations require that your hunting bow be capable of casting a hunting arrow for one hundred and fifty yards, no pulling weight stipulated. Hunting heads must have at least two cutting edges no less than seven-eighths inches in width. Bow must be unstrung while driving. If in a field after dark with a flashlight or spotlight and returning to your car or camp, the bow must be unstrung. When five o'clock comes around, regardless of where I am, I unstring my bow, then I start back for my car. I advise others to do the same. New York regulations are strictly enforced at all times.

New York offers the bowhunter a chance to take two deer legally during one given season. The second deer must be taken in Westchester County, and must be specially tagged as prescribed by the State's Conservation Department. By hunting Westchester County one is able to hunt with the bow up until December 31, which gives one an excellent opportunity to get some hunting done when there's tracking snow.

A special attraction that finds many bowhunters in attendance each year is conducted in Sullivan County at Narrowsburg. This is the annual Bowhunters' Meet, sponsored by the Narrowsburg Chamber of Commerce. The Meet runs for a period of one week during the regular bowhunting season. Awards are given for the largest deer taken during this shindig. Hunting is allowed on all lands owned by both local businessmen and other interested people, and it is very good whitetail country.

There is no special fee required; it is expected that you stay at some local motel or hotel while hunting there. A button is issued for each hunter to wear while hunting, and this permits hunting in many acres on private land. Evenings find a variety of entertainment taking place. The place swarms with bowhunters. So here is a chance to hunt competitively and enjoy some ideal whitetail country.

I saw one of the largest whitetail bucks that I ever hope to see one time when returning from a one-day hunt over a Thanksgiving holiday in New York. While coming down through George

Harriman Park via the White Bear Mountain Bridge after dark, this buck stood in my headlight beams as I approached a turn-off point. I stopped the car to sit and admire this magnificent animal, and drool in agony. I was not able to count his points distinctly but I was sure of at least six on each side, the shortest tine being well over ten inches long. The spread of this buck must have been well over twenty-four inches and the overall height of his rack definitely over thirty inches. He weighed, I judged, at least two hundred and twenty-five pounds on the hoof. Sleek and fat, he stood there feeding away quite unconcerned. I have often wondered what my reactions would be if this buck stepped into view during legal hunting hours in open territory. Such a trophy would be valid reason for a case of buck fever in even the most seasoned hunter.

If you like hunting in mountain terrain with no one to crowd you, the Adirondacks and Catskills provide such country. Whitetails and black bear are abundant in both. And don't forget, they have areas which demand top woodsmanship in which to navigate, both from the standpoint of size and primitive character.

For more information contact State of New York Conservation Department, Albany 1, New York.

Michigan

Michigan, one of our strong contending states in whitetail hunting, offers good bowhunting possibilities, its season lasting thirty-five days from October 1 to November 5. Most parts of the state offer hunter's choice on any sex deer with only a few counties limited to bucks only. In the latter counties, spike bucks with antlers at least three inches long are legal.

Total archery licenses sold in a recent Michigan season were 36,420, and the total estimated kill that year was 1,230 deer. The bowhunter's success ratio, statewide, figures to 3.5 percent with bowhunters spending approximately seven days hunting during the season. A total of 3,777 non-resident bowhunters tried their luck in Michigan the same year.

The county of Allegan, located on the shores of Lake Michigan in the southwest corner of the state, has a bow season open for any sex deer from October 1 to December 15.

Black bear can be taken by archery license holders during the regular season for deer throughout the entire state.

In certain counties, Sunday hunting is prohibited while in others it is permissible with consent of the land owner. Check with the Department of Conservation for the prevailing regulation on this.

State regulations regarding the transporting of a bow in a car require that the bow be unstrung, and that it is enclosed in a case or be carried in the trunk of the car. The taking of a deer for camp use is allowed under special permit and applies during the bowhunting season. Hunting party must number four or more in a camp.

The tab for a non-resident bow and arrow license is fifteen dollars, and the special camp permit for a deer is ten dollars. Camp permit sales were 288, with 130 deer killed in a recent season.

The Michigan terrain offers good whitetail hunting with a mixture of both timber and open areas similar in many ways to the rolling country of its neighboring state Wisconsin, just across the lake. The hot spot for best hunting seems to be in the center state areas classified as Zone Two, where 915 of the total deer kill were accounted for.

Northern counties along Lake Superior in Zone One offer some really wild country for those who want to rough it. Much of this area is not available by road and requires entrance by boat. This area rates second in total deer kill, with the southern counties of Zone Three having the lowest kill.

Archery licenses can be obtained from some four thousand dealers throughout the state or through the main office of the Conservation Department. Anyone desiring additional information on current game regulations or applications for license write to: Michigan Department of Conservation, Lansing 26, Michigan.

Pennsylvania

To those who hail from another state, may I offer the following information concerning the bowhunting potentials in the Keystone State. Sale of archery licenses outnumbers that of any other state with a recent season total sales of 68,051. Hunter success average was 1.7 percent, while those who missed averaged 2.6 trys each. A recent poll conducted by the Game Commission revealed 2,141 archers tried to get their deer. Of these, 85 percent failed, 10 percent hit but did not recover their deer, and 5 percent tagged their venison. Average distance for kills was thirty-two yards. The average time spent hunting was thirty-six hours.

The season opens October 2 and closes October 27. No Sunday hunting is permitted. Daily shooting hours are 6 to 5:30,

E.S.T. Daylight saving time is still in effect during the season, thus actually hunting is legal until 6:30 in the evening. Any deer, regardless of sex or size, is legal.

Non-resident license fee is twenty dollars with an additional cost of two dollars for an archery permit. There are no restrictions on bow weight, arrow shafts, or heads. A strung bow may also be transported in the car during the entire season.

The approximate whitetail herd total numbers well over 100,000. They are found in most counties throughout the state.

The terrain of Pennsylvania offers every type of hunting country that the bowhunter could ask for, from wood-patch hunting in the agricultural areas to rugged mountain hunting in the northern counties.

Northeast areas abound with whitetails in the Pocono Mountain area of Pike, Monroe, and Wayne counties.

Central areas offer good whitetail hunting in the mountain and agricultural areas of Centre, Mifflin, Union, Snyder and Schuylkill counties. Here the big deer of the Blue Mountain area produce many good trophies.

North Central areas of Potter, Tioga, Bradford, Sullivan, Cameron, Clinton, and Lycoming counties offer rugged mountainous hunting country. Located in the rugged mountains of Tioga County is the Grand Canyon of Pennsylvania around the Wellsboro area, where Pine Creek flows south into the broad but rocky Susquehanna River. The hot spot of this area is primitive Potter County with a consistently high total kill season after season.

Northwest areas offer hunting in the mighty Allegheny mountains of Elk, McKean, Warren, Forest, and Clearfield counties. These are the big ones as far as areas with many miles of big, mountainous, timber country are concerned. Also, hunting pressure is the lowest in these counties due to terrain, distance from metropolitan areas, and the vastness of the territory. Here, under the careful control of the Game Commission, lives a wild herd of native elk; protected by closed season, these animals have prospered and propagated under conditions of unlimited range. And when you see a buck in this country, he may be a good one. This is real "compass country" for the stranger.

Visiting bowhunters will find the northeast areas easily available by way of the Northeast extension of the Pennsylvania Turnpike, which cuts through prime whitetail country, the pike ending in Scranton. Good roads lead to every north-central and northwest area; every little mountain hamlet offers tourist accommodations for the hunter.

Bowhunting season finds the hunters well distributed in the many good hunting grounds of the state, with very little crowding in any given area. Perhaps the greatest concentration will be found in the northeast and central and northcentral areas. Pike, Potter, and Schuylkill counties draw the most bowbenders, but there is plenty of elbow room in these hot spots and plenty of deer to go around.

For those who prefer less strenuous hunting, some of the southern counties offer limited whitetails. One can find fair hunting in such counties as Lehigh, Berks, Bucks, Perry, Dauphin, Huntingdon, Blair and Cambria.

The southern side of the Blue Mountain in Lehigh and Berks, Lebanon and Dauphin counties, from Allentown to Harrisburg has produced some tremendous bucks. Fattened on the cultivated crops of farms along the foothills, some of these heads are trophies. Route 22 runs parallel with the Blue Mountains all the way from Allentown into Harrisburg, making it easy to pull off anywhere along the route for good hunting country.

Many acres of state game lands are distributed throughout good hunting country and there are vast acres of state forests. Also, most of the privately-owned land is accessible by getting permission from the owner.

The scenic beauty of Pennsylvania's mountains and the rolling hills of its countryside during the month of October makes it a veritable bowhunter's paradise. The Pennsylvania Dutch cooking for which the state is famous, is a gourmet's delight. Not only do we have big deer, but we also fatten the visiting hunter.

It is not uncommon for the hunter to see as high as twenty to thirty deer per day while hunting in Pennsylvania. The hunter's real problem seems to be in hitting them. Good cover and rugged terrain make for top whitetail hunting while the mild Indian summer days of autumn make it a pleasure.

This is a state of bowhunters, and we are proud of our exceptional safety record during eleven consecutive seasons. We invite you to join us in a hunt at your earliest possible convenience.

New Jersey

New Jersey offers a varied terrain of hunting country for the whitetail bowhunter from the scrub pines of the coastal flats inland to the mountainous country along the east banks of the Delaware River. Deer are quite plentiful in counties bordering on or near the western state line. Central portions of the state offer some good hunting in agricultural areas.

New Jersey requires that a bowhunter pass a test on safety and the proper handling of archery equipment. It is called the "Hunter's Safety Course." A certificate is issued after the test; it must be presented when applying for a license. Instructors appointed by the State Fish and Game Division are found throughout the various counties. No license will be sold to a non-resident applicant without the required certificate to indicate that he or she has passed this course. Once having procured an initial license by passing the "Hunter's Safety Course," the hunter need not take the course each year but may obtain future season licenses upon displaying his last year's license.

A non-resident bowhunting license costs fifteen dollars and fifteen cents. This entitles the hunter to one deer of either sex. The season extends from October 8 to November 11; no Sunday hunting is permitted. A special season of five days follows in December for buck only with antlers of three inches or more being legal. This special season is open for use of both firearms and bow and arrow. Should the bowhunter get his deer during the special bow and arrow season, he may take another deer during the five-day season for firearms. In such a case the second deer, however, must be taken with a firearms hunting license.

Bow and arrow license sales numbered 23,216 resident and 177 nonresident hunters during a recent season, with a reported kill of 1,299. Daily shooting hours are one-half hour before sunrise to one-half hour after sunset.

The most productive counties have been: Hunterdon, Morris, Somerset, and Warren.

Regulations require that any bow used in hunting have a minimum drawing weight of thirty-five pounds and that it be capable of casting a hunting arrow 125 yards to a point of similar elevation. Hunting heads are required to have a minimum width of three-quarters inch, and the maximum width allowed is one and one-half inches. Minimum length of cutting edges of the hunting head must be one and one-half inches, heads must be well sharpened and of metal only. No stipulation is made as to how many cutting edges are required, therefore all types of hunting-head designs are permissible.

Before closing this chapter, I must remind you that the hunting season dates herein indicated for the various states are subject to slight change from year to year.

22

Tomorrow's Controlled Hunting

SINCE most of us who love hunting look forward annually to next year's season with renewed anticipation, it would be well that we think about the future of this big-game hunting we love so much. The embryo hunter stepping into the outdoors for his initial year of hunting pleasure and experiences with whitetail deer quickly becomes one of the "can't wait until next season" dedicated hunters. But the youngster beginning his hunting experiences today faces future hunting which will be of a decidedly different character than we have enjoyed in the past.

The population explosion experienced by our nation in the past ten years has had a decided effect on the future big-game hunting potential. The most important factor influencing future hunting is the status of the deer herd. In Pennsylvania, for example, it is my opinion that we have reached a peak of permissible deer population. Certain increasing pressures demand an inevitable and drastic reduction of the herd's total size. Simultaneously, the ever increasing annual sale of hunting licenses indicates mounting hunting pressure. The ratio of hunters to available deer will shortly exceed that which can be met from a practicable standpoint by even the most efficient game management methods.

The highly effective management of our deer herds in the past fifteen years is most laudatory. Informed game management has produced whitetails in such abundance that the Pennsylvania hunter now enjoys big-game hunting surpassing that of any previous year.

But as is too often the case, this state of "Utopia" has its shortcoming. Drastic reduction of the herd is now imperative because of the lack of enough good range to support it.

With the Game Commission fully aware of this problem, a carefully planned program of special, controlled antlerless deer seasons has been inaugurated. These seasons have been highly effective for several years and their use in big-game management undoubtedly will not only be continued, but even expanded.

The loss of huge acreages of land each year to both residential construction and industrial expansion seriously affects the future of our whitetail. Much of the land absorbed in urban development was deer range. This steady disappearance of huge tracts of land robs the whitetail of its most vital necessity, proper feed in ample abundance. It also means an increasing lack of adequate cover for the present whitetail population. Experience during extreme winter seasons clearly indicates that artificial feeding is an impossibility from both the financial and manpower standpoints.

Drastic reduction in herd number, therefore, is the only solution tô this grim but very real problem. Our shrinking hunting grounds do not permit any alternatives. Conservation experts and the best game management men cannot otherwise cope with it. With the fate of the deer herd so clearly discernible for the future, hunting is bound to be directly affected and changes must occur.

I expect to see controlled hunting come into being in due time, not by choice but by virtue of absolutely necessity. The drawing of a given number of permits will then allow so many lucky ones to hunt for that particular season, while the balance of hunter applicants will have to wait for the next year's drawing. This may sound extreme to many hunters. But bear in mind that this method has been practiced by certain states for some years where the species are limited. Such a system permits a few hunters to harvest only a limited number of surplus animals and thus reduces the herd to that given number of game animals which can be accommodated by the amount and quality of available range and feed. So this, then, means that the future hunter, the unborn generations if not our children, face lean years of deer hunting as compared to past bounty.

The ever expanding residential and industrial growth of our country brings about another problem which affects the big-game hunter. This is a constant reduction in the number of areas in which the high-power hunting rifle can be safely used. This suggests other potential changes in our future hunting privileges. It might well mean, for example, restricting the use of long-range weapons and as compelling the use of short-range firearms only. This evolution may probably take place by regulations first stepping down big-game ammunition to the rifled shotgun slug, and then perhaps eventually even a reduction to spread shot. We must also realize that another pressure factor that may require this reduction of firepower will be the ever increasing number of hunters who go afield each year. Actually, we are putting more men into a lesser area each year, and this presents severe problems in terms of safety.

From the standpoint of regulation, of all the several deer hunter classifications today, the bowhunter seems to stand the most chance of surviving with his weapon. Short-range effectiveness and killing power permits the bow's use in smaller geographic areas than any type of firearm.

Westchester County in New York State is an excellent example to illustrate this point. With suburban development throughout the County reducing hunting grounds to patches of only a few acres, the use of firearms would be highly dangerous. While the whitetail has learned to live among the estates and the County's network of back roads, his number has been carefully kept within proper limits by an annual bowhunting season. This is the only hunting weapon allowed during the County's deer seasons. I expect to see much similar regulation take place in some of our counties in Pennsylvania and other states within the next ten years.

Note also that with the bow used as the only hunting weapon, seasons can be wisely extended for longer periods of time, thus allowing more hunters to enjoy several days of hunting each year. Since recreation and relaxation are the greatest objectives anyway for most bowhunters, the fact that no great quantities of game are taken will not adversely affect hunter morale nor discourage participation.

With this somewhat pessimistic prediction, perhaps, concerning the future of deer hunting, it is only natural to include a prognostication that in the future only the most skilled will bring home the venison. Therefore, it is my sincere hope that the chapters in this book will prove beneficial to some; I use the term "some," realizing that not everyone who will buy an archery permit is necessarily bent on becoming a real "dyed in the wool" bowhunter.

Hunting, without any doubt, is a contest between animal and man. The competition involves the animal's natural instinct for survival against the hunter's degree of skill. But many who go bowhunting each year lack any appreciable knowledge of the whitetail they hope to kill. Although they are highly capable in handling the bow, they place no importance on knowing their game. Some of these hunters do get their deer, but their good fortune definitely arises from pure luck in most instances.

When a man becomes really interested in any hobby, he strives to improve his knowledge of his chosen relaxation constantly. He makes use of available information and educates himself towards greater proficiency. Thus he derives a greater satisfaction in his participation. Yes, hobbies are fine for relaxation and recreation, but inadequate background and lack of skill often lead to frustration.

The man who chooses hunting as his hobby finds it a demanding pastime. To hunt properly one must work hard. The successful hunter with his own trophy racks on a den wall will tell you they did not come easy. Neither did that real trophy buck just grow that big by frequenting the roadside and open fields. Most such heads demand that the hunter search for them in real "back in" hunting country. It takes the proper planning of a hunt, complete whitetail "know how," and a fair degree of skill with the bow to obtain really good trophy heads.

Civilization with all its conveniences has made many a man a cliff dweller. The crowded cities and the hustle of progress increasingly separate man from the outdoors. No wonder the real bowhunter talks, eats, sleeps, and lives for each hunting season. To be alone in the vast quiet of the forest on some deer stand is the kind of tonic every bowhunter needs in order that he may survive the long cold winter! And the serenity of good hunting country gives the bowhunter a chance for closer contact with himself; mental relaxation presides during any good hunt. That's why I am quite sure no man will ever suffer a nervous breakdown or develop a case of ulcers purely as the result of his hunting activities.

So here is a prescription to benefit any man. Buy a bow, arrows, and an archery permit. Take a few days of vacation this fall for whitetail hunting. You will return a better man, indeed, and in most cases, a far wiser one.

When the Game Warden up above decides to place his big-game tag on me, I hope I will be led to some whitetail stand in the hereafter midst the solemn oak and mountain fern, where peace and quiet reign supreme. Until then, may good hunting be your pleasure. May your shafts speed true and your misses be but few.